주역 周易

주역

옮 김 卞廷煥
펴낸이 이준구
펴낸곳 대구한의대학교출판부
712-715 경북 경산시 한의대로 1번지
Tel (053) 819-1577

초판 발행 2010년 6월 28일
2 판 발행 2011년 8월 24일

ISBN 978-89-87696-75-1 93150

가격은 뒤표지에 있습니다.

주역

卞廷煥 옮김

대구한의대학교출판부

역자 서문

인간이 걸어가야 할 바른 도리가 담겨 있다

『주역周易』은 『시경詩經』, 『서경書經』과 더불어 동양 고전에서 으뜸을 차지하는 경전이다. 또한 『주역周易』은 복희씨, 문왕, 주공, 공자 4성인의 합작품이며 성인이 직접 집필한 것으로는 최초이다. 고대 중국인들의 삶이 용해되어 있는 지혜의 보고寶庫이자, 유가의 기본경전인 사서삼경四書三經, 십삼경十三經 가운데 하나로 존중되는 책이다. 『주역』에는 우주만물의 운행 법칙이 담겨 있을 뿐만 아니라, 인간이 걸어가야 할 바른 도리가 포함되어 있다. 그래서 『주역』은 일반적으로 대자연과 인간을 일관하는 진리를 밝힌 책으로 간주된다.

『주역』은 본래 불안한 미래를 알아보려는 동기에서 만들어진 점서占書였다. 복잡다단한 현실은 언제나 현명한 선택을 위한 지혜를 요구하였고, 『주역』은 끊임없이 운동·변화하는 대우주의 법칙성에 근거하여 그 해답을 제공하려 하였다. 무수한 별의 움직임 가운데 정연한 궤도가 있고, 사계절의 변화 가운데 일정한 주기가 있는 것처럼, 『주역』은 자연계의 법칙성에 근거하여 인간생활에 유용한 예지를 전해주려 하였다.

『주역』에서는 기본적으로 우주의 삼라만상이 발생하고 소멸하는 이치와, 복잡하게 전개되는 양상을, 음陰과 양陽이라는 두 기운이 착종한 결과로 본다. 그리고 세상에서 발생하는 수많은 사태를 축약하여 64개의 괘(유형)로 만들었고, 나아가 그 우주자연의 원리에 근거하여 소우주라고 할 인간의 운명에 적용하였다. 이처럼 자연의 원리에 근거하여 인간의 원리를 세우려는 인간의 삶의 현상 가운데 대우주의 법칙성이 내재되어 있다고 보기 때문이다.

인간의 삶은 과거와 현재와 미래로 이루어진 항등식으로 볼 수 있다. X + Y = Z라는 항등식에서, 과거인 X에 현재인 Y를 대입하면 미래인 Z를 알 수 있다. 그러기에 『주역』은 명리학命理學을 하는 사람에게 최고의 교범으로 여겨진다. 그렇지만 『주역』은 단지 점서에만 머무르지 않고, 생활에 대한 온갖 지혜, 특히 수양과 처세를 위한 지침을 내포하고 있다.

최근 『주역』에 담겨있는 원리가 천체물리학, 유전공학 등의 첨단 과학의 성과와도 부합한다고 알려지고 있다. 또한 『주역』이 포함하는 조화의 원리, 정반합의 원리는 현대인이 당면한 자연과 인간의 불화, 인간의 존엄성 상실 등의 문제에도 유용한 것으로 평가되고 있다. 역자는 어릴 때부터 이 책을 애독해 왔으며, 지금도 반복해서 읽고 사색하여 깊은 깨달음을 얻고 있다. 독자들도 이 책을 통해 역자가 느꼈던 기쁨을 만끽하기를 희망한다.

2010. 2. 역자 변정환

차례

주역 上經

주역 下經

❖ F(first)9는 初九(초구)를 말한다.
❖ 92는 九二(구이)를 말한다.
❖ 93은 九三(구삼)을 말한다.
❖ 94는 九四(구사)를 말한다.
❖ 95는 九五(구오)를 말한다.
❖ 96은 九六(구육)을 말한다.
❖ L(last)9는 上九(상구)를 말한다.
❖ U(used)9는 用九(용구)를 말한다.

주역

上經

乾

天重 乾 一

乾、元、亨、利、貞。

初九、潛龍、勿用。

九二、見龍在田、利見大人。

九三、君子終日乾乾、夕惕若、厲、无咎。

九四、或躍在淵、无咎。

九五、飛龍在天、利見大人。

上九、亢龍、有悔。

用九、見羣龍、无首、吉。

象曰、大哉 乾元。萬物 資始 乃統天。雲行雨施 品物、流形。大明終始 六位時成 時乘六龍 以御天。乾道變化 各正性命、保合太和、乃利貞。首出庶物 萬國 咸寧。

象曰、天行 健、君子 以 自强不息。潛龍勿用 陽在下也、見龍在田 德施普也。終日乾乾 反復道也。或躍或淵、進、无咎也。飛龍在天 大人造也。亢龍有悔 盈不可久也。用九、天德、不可爲首也。

건乾은 크고 형통하며 이롭고 바르다.

초9는 물 속에 잠겨 있는 용이니 쓰지 말라.

92는 용이 밭에 나타났으니 대인을 만남이 이롭다.

93은 군자가 종일토록 굳세고 굳세게 해서 저녁에 두려워하면 비록 위태로우나 허물은 없을 것이다.

94는 혹 뛰어 연못에 있으면 허물이 없을 것이다.

95는 나는 용이 하늘에 있으니 대인大人을 만남이 이롭다.

상9는 지나친 용이니 후회가 있을 것이다.

용9는 뭇 용을 보되, 우두머리가 없으면 길한 것이다.

Qian represents what is great and originating, penetrating, advantageous, correct and firm.

1. F9, undivided, we see its subject as the dragon lying hid in the deep. It is not the time for active doing.
2. 92, undivided, we see its subject as the dragon appearing in the field. It will be advantageous to meet with the great man.
3. 93, undivided, we see its subject as the superior man active and vigilant all the day, and in the evening still careful and apprehensive. The position is dangerous, but there will be no mistake.
4. 94, we see its subject as the dragon looking as if he were leaping up, but still in the deep. There will be no mistake.
5. 95, undivided, we see its subject as the dragon on the wing in the sky. It will be advantageous to meet with the great man.
6. L9, undivided, we see its subject as the dragon exceeding the proper limits. There will be occasion for repentance.
7. U9, undivided, as appears from the use of the number nine. If the host of dragons thus appearing were to divest themselves of their heads, there would be good fortune.

文言傳

文言曰、元者、善之長也、亨者、嘉之會也、利者、義之和也、貞者、事之幹也。君子體仁、足以長人、嘉會足以合禮、利物足以和義、貞固足以幹事。君子行此四德者。故曰乾元亨利貞。

初九曰、潛龍勿用、何謂也。子曰龍德而隱者也、不易乎世、不成乎名、遯世无悶、不見是而无悶、樂則行之、憂則違之、確乎其不可拔、潛龍也。

九二曰、見龍在田利見大人、何謂也。子曰龍德而正中者也、庸言之信、庸行之謹、閑邪存其誠、善世而不伐、德博而化、易曰見龍在田利見大人、君德也。

九三曰、君子終日乾乾夕惕若厲无咎、何謂也。子曰君子進德修業、忠信、所以進德也、修辭立其誠、所以居業也。知至至之、可與幾也、知終終之、可與存義也。是故、居上位不驕、在下位而不憂。故、乾乾、因其時而惕、雖危、无咎矣。

「문언文言」에서 말하기를, 원元은 착한 것의 으뜸이요, 형亨은 아름다움의 모임이요, 이利는 의로움의 조화요, 정貞은 일의 주관이다. 군자는 인을 체득하여 사람들을 길러주며, 아름다움이 모이면 예를 합당하게 되며, 사물을 이롭게 하되 의로움에 조화되도록 하며, 바르게 굳게 일을 주관한다. 군자가 이 네 가지 덕을 행하는 자이다. 그러므로 "건은 원형이정이다"라고 말한다.
초9에서 '잠용물용潛龍勿用'이라 함은 무엇을 말하는가?

What is called under Qian 'the great and originating' is in man the first and chief quality of goodness; what is called 'the penetrating' is the assemblage of excellences; what is called 'the advantageous' is the harmony of all that is right; and what is called 'the correct and firm' is the faculty of action. The superior man, embodying benevolence, is fit to preside over men; presenting the assemblage of excellences, he is fit to show in himself the union of all propriety; benefiting all creatures, he is fit to exhibit the harmony of all that is right; correct and firm, he is fit to manage all affairs. The fact that the superior man practises these four virtues justifies the application to him of the words— 'Qian represents what is great and originating, penetrating, advantageous, correct and firm.'
What is the meaning of the words under F9, undivided, 'The dragon lies hid in the deep;—it is not the time for active doing?'

공자가 말씀하시길, 용의 덕을 지녔으나, 숨은 자이니, 세상에 의해 바뀌지 않으며, 이름을 이루지 못하여 세상과 동떨어져 있어도 근심하지 않으며, 옳음을 보지 못해도 근심하지 않으며, 즐거우면 행하고 걱정스러우면 어기니, 확고하게 움직일 수 없음이 '잠용'이다.
92에 이르기를 "현룡재전見龍在田, 이견대인利見大人"이라 한 것은 무엇을 말하는가? 공자가 말씀하시길, 용의 덕을 지니고 정중正中한 자이니, 평소의 말이 믿음직스러우며, 평소의 행동이 신중하며, 간사한 것을 막고 성실함을 보존하며,

The Master said: —'There he is, with the powers of the dragon, and yet lying hid. The influence of the world would make no change in him; he would do nothing merely to secure his fame. He can live, withdrawn from the world, without regret; he can experience disapproval without trouble of mind. Rejoicing in opportunity, he carries his principles into action; sorrowing for want of opportunity, he keeps with them in retirement. Yes, he is not to be torn from his root in himself.' This is 'the dragon lying hid.'
What is the meaning of the world under 92, 'The dragon shows himself and is in the field; —it will be advantageous to see the great man?' The Master said: —'There he is, with the dragon's powers, and occupying exactly the central place. He is sincere even in his ordinary words, and earnest in his ordinary conduct. Guarding against depravity, he preserves his sincerity.

세상에 선을 떨쳐도 자랑하지 않으며, 덕이 널리 펴지고 교화되니, 역에서 말하기를, "현룡재전, 이견대인"이라 하니, 임금의 덕이다.
93에 이르기를, "군자종일건건君子終日乾乾, 석척약려무구夕惕若厲无咎"라고 한 것은 무엇을 말하는가? 공자가 말씀하시길, 군자가 덕을 행하고 공업功業을 닦으니, 충실하고 신실함은 덕을 행하는 것이요, 말을 닦고 그 정성을 들임이 공업을 이루는 까닭이다. 앎이 지극하여 지극함에 도달하니, 사물의 기미를 파악하며, 끝을 알아서 마치니, 의로움을 간직할 수 있다.

His goodness is recognised in the word, but he does not boast of it. His virtue is extensively displayed, and transformation ensues. The language of the Yi, "The dragon shows himself and is in the field; —it will be advantageous to see the great man," refers to a ruler's virtue.'
What is the meaning of the words under 93, 'The superior man is active and vigilant all the day, and in the evening still careful and apprehensive; —the position is dangerous, but there will be no mistake?' The Master said: —'The superior man advances in virtue, and cultivates all the sphere of his duty. His leal-heartedness and good faith are the way by which he advances in virtue. His attention to his words and establishing his sincerity are the way by which he occupies in his sphere. He knows the utmost point to be reached, and reaches it, thus showing himself in accord with the first springs of things; he knows the end to be rested in, and rests in it, thus preserving his righteousness in accordance with that end.

九四曰、或躍在淵无咎、何謂也。子曰上下无常、非爲邪也、進退无恒、非離群也。君子進德修業、欲及時也。故、无咎。

九五曰、飛龍在天利見大人、何謂也。子曰同聲相應、同氣相求、水流濕、火就燥、雲從龍、風從虎。聖人、作而萬物、覩、本乎天者、親上、本乎地者、親下、則各從其類也。

上九曰、亢龍有悔、何謂也。子曰貴而无位、高而无民、賢人、在下位而无輔。是以動而有悔也。

潛龍勿用、下也、見龍在田、時舍也、終日乾乾、行事也、或躍在淵、自試也、飛龍在天、上治也、亢龍有悔、窮之災也、乾元用九、天下治也。

潛龍勿用、陽氣潛藏、見龍在田、天下文明、終日乾乾與時偕行、或躍在淵、乾道乃革、飛龍在大、乃位乎天德、亢龍有悔、與時偕極、乾元用九、乃見天則。

이런 까닭에 윗자리에 있어도 교만하지 않으며, 아랫자리에 있어도 근심하지 않는다. 그러므로 굳세고 굳세어서 그 때에 따라 두려워하면 비록 위태로우나 허물이 없을 것이다.
94에서 "혹약재연무구或躍在淵无咎"라고 한 것을 무엇을 말하는가? 공자가 말씀하시길, 오르내림에 항상함이 없음은 간사함을 행하는 것이 아니며, 나아가고 물러감이 일정하지 않음은 무리를 떠나려는 것이 아니다. 군자가 진덕수업進德修業하는 것은 그 때에 맞게 하고자 함이다. 그러므로 허물이 없다.
95에서 "비룡재천飛龍在天, 이견대인利見大人"이란 한 것은 무엇을 말하는가?

Therefore he occupies a high position without pride, and low position without anxiety. Thus it is that, being active and vigilant, and careful also and apprehensive as the time requires, though his position be perilous, he will make no mistake.'
What is the meaning of the words under 94, 'He is as if he were leaping up, but still is in the deep;—there will be no mistake?' The Master said:—'He finds no permanent place either above or below, but he does not commit the error of advancing. He may advance or recede;—there is no permanent place for him: but he does not leave his fellows. The superior man, advancing in virtue and cultivating the sphere of his duty, yet wishes to advance only at the proper time, and therefore there is no mistake.'
What is the meaning of the words under 95, 'The dragon is on the wing in the sky;—it will be advantageous to see the great man?'

공자가 말씀하시길, 같은 소리가 서로 응하고 같은 기운이 서로 구하여 물은 젖은 데로 흐르고 불은 마른 데로 나아가며 구름은 용을 좇고 바람은 범을 좇는다. 성인이 일어남에 만물이 바라보니, 하늘에 근본한 자는 위로 친하고 땅에 근본한 자는 아래로 친하니 곧 각자 같은 무리를 좇는다.
상9에서 '항용유회亢龍有悔'라 한 것은 무엇을 말하는가? 공자가 말씀하시길, 귀해도 자리가 없으며, 높아도 백성이 없으며, 현인은 아랫 자리에 있어도 도움이 없다. 이로써 움직임에 후회가 있다.

The Master said: —'Notes of the same key respond to one another; creatures of the same nature seek one another; water flows towards the place that is low and damp; fire rises up towards what is dry; clouds follow the dragon, and winds follow the tiger: —so the sage makes his appearance, and all men look to him. Things that draw their origin from heaven move towards what is above; things that draw their origin from the earth cleave to what is below: —so does everything follow its kind.'
What is the meaning of the words under L9, 'The dragon exceeds the proper limits; —there will be occasion for repentance?'
The Master said: —'The position is noble, but it is not that of office; its occupant dwells on high, but he has no people to rule; and the men of talent and virtue in the positions below will give him no aid; —should he move in such a case, there will be occasion for repentance.'

'잠룡물용潛龍勿用'은 낮춤이요, '현룡재전見龍在田'은 때로 통함이요, '종일건건終日乾乾'은 그 일을 행함이요, '혹약재연或躍在淵'은 스스로를 시험함이요, '비룡재천飛龍在天'은 위에서 다스림이요, '항룡유회亢龍有悔'는 궁한 재앙이요, '건원용구乾元用九'는 천하를 다스리는 것이다.
'잠룡물용'은 양기가 잠겨서 숨어 있음이요, '현룡재전'은 천하가 문채롭고 밝음이요,

'The dragon lies hid; —it is not the time for active doing:' —the position is too low. 'The dragon shows himself and is in the field:' —the time requires him still to be unemployed. 'All the day active and vigilant:' —he now does his proper business. 'He is as if he were leaping up, but still is in the deep:' —he is making trial of himself. 'The dragon is on the wing in the sky:' —the subject of the line is on high and ruling. 'The dragon exceeds the proper limit, and there will be occasion for repentance:' —when things have been carried to extremity, calamity ensues. Undivided lines appear in all these representations of the great and originating power denoted by Qian: —what follows in the Yao tells us how all under the sky there will be good order.
'The dragon lies hid in the deep; —it is not the time for active doing:' —the energy denoted by the undivided line is laid up and hid away as in the deep. 'The dragon appears in the field:' —all under heaven begins to be adorned and brightened.

乾元者、始而亨者也、利貞者、性情也。乾始能以美利、利天下。不言所利、大矣哉。大哉、乾乎。剛健中正純粹、精也。六爻發揮、旁通情也、時乘六龍 以御天也、雲行雨施、天下平也。

君子以成德爲行、日可見之、行也。潛之爲言也、隱而未見 行而未成。是以君子弗用也。君子學以聚之、問以辨之、寬以居之、仁以行之、易曰 見龍在田利見大人、君德也。

九三 重剛而不中、上不在天、下不在田。故、乾乾、因其時而惕、雖危、无咎矣。

九四 重剛而不中、上不在天、下不在田、中不在人、故、或之、或之者疑之也、故、无咎。

夫大人者、與天地合其德、與日月合其明、與四時合其序、與鬼神合其吉凶、先天而天弗違、後天而奉天時、天且弗違、而況於人乎。況於鬼神乎。亢之爲言也、知進而不知退、知存而不知亡、知得而不知喪、其唯聖人乎。知進退存亡而不失其正者、其唯聖人乎。

'종일건건'은 때로 더불어 함께 행함이요, '혹약재연'은 건의 도가 바뀜이요, '비룡재천'은 천하의 덕에 자리하는 것이요, '항룡유회'는 때와 함께 다함이요, '건원용구'는 하늘의 법칙을 봄이다.
건의 원元은 시작해서 형통함이요, 이롭고 바른 것은 정情과 성性이다. 건의 비롯함은 아름다운 이로움으로써 천하를 이롭게 한다. 이로운 것을 말하지 않으니 크도다.

'All the day active and vigilant:'—continually, as the time passes and requires, does he act. 'He is as if he were leaping up, but still is in the deep:'—a change is taking place in the method indicated by this Qian diagram. 'The dragon is on the wing in the sky:'—this shows that his place is based on his heavenly virtue. 'The dragon exceeds the proper limit;—there will be occasion for repentance:'—the time is come to an end, and so also is his opportunity. Undivided NINES appear in all these representations of the great and originating power denoted by Qian:—and from what follows in the Yao we see the model of action afforded by heaven.
The 'greatness' and 'originating' represented by Qian refer to it as the symbol of what gives their beginning to all things, and also secures their growth and development. 'The advantageousness and the correctness and firmness' refer to its nature and feelings as seen in all the resulting things. Qian, thus originating, is able with its admirable benefits to benefit all under the sky. We are not told how its benefits are conferred; but how great is its operation!

크도다, 건이여! 강건하고 중정中正하며 순수함은 정미함이요, 여섯 효가 발휘하는 것은 두루 실정에 통함이요, 때로 여섯 용을 타서 하늘을 부리니, 구름이 일어나 비가 내리니, 천하가 태평하다.
군자는 덕을 이룸으로써 행동으로 삼으니, 날로 보이는 것이 행동이다. 용이 물 속에 잠겨있다고 말한 것은 숨어서 나타나지 않으며, 행함이 이루어지지 않는 것이다. 그러므로 군자가 쓰지 않는다. 군자는 배움으로써 모으고 물어서 분별하며, 너그러움으로써 거주하고 어짊으로써 행하니,

How great is what is emblemed by Qian! —strong, vigorous, undeflected, correct, and in all these qualities pure, unmixed, exquisite! The six lines, as explained by the duke of Zhou, bring forth and display its meaning, and everything about it is thus indirectly exhibited. The great man at the proper time drives with these six dragons through the sky. The clouds move, and the rain is distributed; all under heaven enjoys repose.
In the superior man his conduct is the fruit of his perfected virtue, which might be seen therefore in his daily course; but the force of that phrase, 'lying hid,' requires him to keep retired, and not yet show himself, nor proceed to the full development of his course. While this is the case, the superior man knows that it is not the time for active doing. The superior man learns and accumulates the results of his learning; puts questions, and discriminates among those results; dwells magnanimously and unambitiously in what he has attained to; and carries it into practice with benevolence.

역易에서 "현룡재전見龍在田, 이견대인利見大人"이라 이르니, 군자의 덕이다.
93은 거듭 강하지만 가운데 있지 않아서, 위로는 하늘에 있지 않고 아래로는 밭에 있지 않다. 그러므로 굳세고 굳세어서 그 때를 따라서 두려워하면 비록 위태로우나 허물은 없을 것이다.
94는 거듭 강하지만 가운데 있지 않아서 위로는 하늘에 있지 않고 아래로는 밭에 있지 않으며, 가운데로 사람에게 있지 않다. 그러므로 '혹或'이라고 하니, 혹이라는 것은 의심하는 것이다. 그러므로 허물이 없다.

What the Yi says, 'The dragon appears in the field: —it will be advantageous to meet with the great man,' has reference to the virtuous qualities of a ruler as thus described.
In 93, there is a twofold symbol of strength, but the position is not central. Its occupant is not in heaven above, nor is he in the field beneath. Therefore there must be active vigilance and cautious apprehension as the time requires; and though the position be perilous, there will be no mistake.
In 94, there is the symbol of strength, but the position is not central. Its occupant is not in heaven above, nor is he in the field beneath, nor is he in the place of man intermediate. Hence he is in perplexity; and being so, he has doubts about what should be his movements, and so will give no occasion for blame.

저 대인은 하늘과 땅과 더불어 그 덕을 같이 하고, 해와 달과 더불어 그 밝음을 같이 하며, 사시四時와 더불어 그 차례를 같이 하고, 귀신과 더불어 그 길흉을 같이하며, 하늘보다 앞서더라도 하늘이 어기지 않고, 하늘보다 뒤지더라도 하늘의 때를 받드니, 하늘도 또한 어기지 아니하는데, 하물며 사람이며 하물며 귀신이랴. 높다고 말하는 것은, 나아가는 것만 알고, 물러설 줄을 모르고, 얻는 것만 알고 없어짐을 모르며, 얻음을 알고 잃음을 모르니, 그 오직 성인뿐인가? 진퇴존망을 알아서 그 바름을 잃지 않는 자는 오직 성인뿐일 것이다!

The great man is he who is in harmony, in his attributes, with heaven and earth; in his brightness, with the sun and moon; in his orderly procedure, with the four seasons; and in his relation to what is fortunate and what is calamitous, in harmony with the spirit-like operations of Providence. He may precede Heaven, and Heaven will not act in opposition to him; he may follow Heaven, but will act only as Heaven at the time would do. If Heaven will not act in opposition to him, how much less will men! how much less will the spirit-like operation of Providence! The force of that phrase—'exceeding the proper limits'—indicates the knowing to advance but not to retire; to maintain but not to let perish; to get but not to lose. He only is the sage who knows to advance and to retire, to maintain and to let perish; and that without ever acting incorrectly. Yes, he only is the sage!

地重 ䷁ 坤 ②

坤、元、亨、利牝馬之貞。君子有攸往、先、迷、後、得主利。西南得朋、東北、喪朋。安貞、吉。

象曰、至哉、坤元、萬物、資生、乃順承天。坤厚載物、德合无疆、含弘光大、品物、咸亨。牝馬、地類、行地无疆、柔順利貞。君子攸行、先、迷、失道、後、順、得常。西南得朋、乃與類行、東北喪朋、乃終有慶。安貞之吉、應地无疆。

象曰、地勢坤、君子以、厚德、載物。

初六、履霜、堅冰、至。象曰、履霜堅冰、陰始凝也、馴致其道、至堅冰也。

六二、直方大、不習、无不利。象曰、六二之動、直以方也、不習无不利、地道光也。

六三、含章可貞、或從王事、无成有終。象曰、含章可貞、以時發也、或從王事、知光大也。

六四、括囊、无咎、无譽。象曰、括囊无咎、愼不害也。

六五、黃裳、元吉。象曰、黃裳元吉、文在中也。

上六、龍戰于野、其血、玄黃。象曰、龍戰于野、其道窮也。

用六、利永貞。象曰、用六永貞、以大終也。

곤坤은 크게 형통하고, 암말의 곧음이 이로우니, 군자가 갈 바가 있다. 앞서면 길을 잃고 뒤따르면 주군을 얻어 이롭다. 서남쪽은 벗을 얻고 동북쪽은 벗을 잃으니, 편안하게 곧아서 길할 것이다.

초6은 서리를 밟으면 굳은 얼음이 이른다.
62는 곧고 반듯하고 크므로, 익히지 않아도 이롭지 않음이 없다.
63은 빛나는 것을 머금어 곧게 지키는 것이니, 혹은 왕王의 일을 따라 이룸은 없으나 마침은 있다.
64는 주머니를 홀치는 것이니 허물도 없고 명예도 없다.
65는 누런 치마면 크게 길할 것이다.
상6은 용이 들에서 싸우니 그 피가 검고 누렇다.
용6은 영원히 곧음이 이롭다.

Kun represents what is great and originating, penetrating, advantageous, correct and having the firmness of a mare. When the superior man here intended has to make any movement, if he take the initiative, he will go astray; if he follow, he will find his proper lord. The advantageousness will be seen in his getting friends in the south-west, and losing friends in the north-east. If he rest in correctness and firmness, there will be good fortune.

1. F6, divided, we see its subject treading on hoarfrost. The strong ice will come by and by.
2. 62, divided, shows the attribute of being straight, square, and great. Its operation, without repeated efforts, will be in every respect advantageous.
3. 63, divided, shows its subject keeping his excellence under restraint, but firmly maintaining it. If he should have occasion to engage in the king's service, though he will not claim the success for himself, he will bring affairs to a good issue.
4. 64, divided, shows the symbol of a sack tied up. There will be no ground for blame or for praise.
5. 65, divided, shows the yellow lower garment. There will be great good fortune.
6. L6, divided shows dragons fighting in the wild. Their blood is purple and yellow.
7. U6, divided, as appears from the use of the number SIX. If those who are thus represented be perpetually correct and firm, advantage will arise.

文言傳

文言曰、坤 至柔而動也剛、至靜而德方、後得、主利而有常 含萬物而化光、
坤道其順乎。承天而時行。

積善之家、必有餘慶、積不善之家、必有餘殃、臣弑其君 子弑其父 非一朝一
夕之故。其所由來者、漸矣、由辨之不早辨也、易曰 履霜堅氷至、蓋言順也。

直、其正也、方、其義也、君子敬以直內、義以方外、敬義立而德不孤、直方
大不習无不利、則不疑其所行也。

陰雖有美、含之、以從王事、弗敢成也、地道也、妻道也、臣道也、地道、无
成而代有終也。天地變化、草木蕃 天地閉、賢人、隱。易曰 括囊无咎无譽
蓋言謹也。

君子黃中通理、正位居體、美在其中而暢於四支、發於事業 美之至也。陰疑
於陽、必戰、爲其嫌於无陽也。故、稱龍焉、猶未離其類也。故、稱血焉、
夫玄黃者、天地之雜也 天玄而地黃。

「문언文言」에서 말하기를, 곤은 지극히 부드럽지만 움직임은 강하고, 지극히 조용하지만 덕은 반듯하니, 뒤에 얻어도 주인이 이롭고 일정함이 있으며, 만물을 머금어 조화가 빛나니, 곤의 도는 유순한 것인저. 하늘을 이어받아 때에 알맞게 행한다.
선을 쌓은 집에는 반드시 경사가 넘치고 불선을 쌓은 집에는 반드시 재앙이 넘칠 것이니, 신하가 임금을 시해하고 자식이 아버지를 시해하는 일은 하루아침에 벌어지는 일이 아니다. 그 연유한 바가 점차로 이뤄진 것이다. 분별할 것을 일찍 분별하지 못함으로 말미암은 것이니, 역에서 말하기를, "서리를 밟으면 굳은 얼음이 이른다" 하였으니, 대개 손순함을 말한 것이다.

What is indicated by Kun is most gentle and weak, but, when put in motion, is hard and strong; it is most still, but is able to give every definite form. 'By following, it obtains its proper lord,' and pursues its regular course. It contains all things in itself, and its transforming power is glorious. Yes, what docility marks the way of Kun! It receives the influences of heaven, and acts at the proper time.
The family that accumulates goodness is sure to have superabundant happiness, and the family that accumulates evil is sure to have superabundant misery. The murder of a ruler by his minister, or of his father by a son, is not the result of the events of one morning or one evening. The causes of it have gradually accumulated,—through the absence of early discrimination. The words of the Yi, 'He treads on the hoar-frost; the strong ice will come by and by,' show the natural issue and growth of things.

직直은 바름이요, 방方은 의로움이니, 군자는 공경으로써 안을 바르게 하고, 의로움으로써 밖을 반듯하게 하여, 공경과 의로움을 세워 덕이 외롭지 않으니, "직방대直方大, 불습무불리不習无不利"라고 한 것은 곧 그 행하는 바를 의심하지 않음을 말한 것이다.
음이 비록 아름다우나 머금어서 왕의 일을 좇아 감히 이루지 못하니, 이는 땅의 도이고, 부인의 도이며, 신하의 도이니, 땅의 도는 이룸이 없고, 대신 마침을 둔다. 천지가 변화하면 초목이 번성하고 천지가 폐장하면 현인이 숨는다.

'Straight' indicates the correctness of the internal principle, and 'square,' the righteousness of the external act. The superior man, thus represented, by his self-reverence maintains the inward correctness, and in righteousness adjusts his external acts. His reverence and righteousness being thus established, his virtues are not solitary instances or of a single class. 'Straight, square, and great, working his operations, without repeated efforts, in every respect advantageous:'—this shows how such a one has no doubts as to what he does.
Although the subject of this divided line has excellent qualities, he does not display them, but keeps them under restraint. 'If he engage with them in the service of the king, and be successful, he will not claim that success for himself:'—this is the way of the earth, of a wife, of a minister. The way of the earth is—'not to claim the merit of achievement,' but on behalf of heaven to bring things to their proper issue. Through the changes and transformations produced by heaven and earth, plants and trees grow luxuriantly. If the reciprocal influence of heaven and earth were shut up and restrained, we should have a state that might suggest to us the case of men of virtue and ability lying in obscurity.

역에서 말하기를, "괄낭括囊, 무구무예无咎无譽"라고 한 것은 대개 삼가라는 말이다.
군자가 한가운데서 이치에 통달하고 바른 자리에서 몸에 거하여 아름다움이 그 가운데에 있어 사지에 빛나며 사업에서 발휘되니 지극한 아름다움이다. 음이 양을 의심하면 반드시 싸우니 그 양이 없음을 싫어하기 때문이다. 그러므로 용을 말했고, 오히려 그 무리를 떠나지 못함이다. 그러므로 피를 말했으니, 저 검고 누른 것은 천지가 섞인 것이니 하늘은 검고 땅은 누렇다.

The words of the Yi, 'A sack tied up:—there will be no ground for blame or for praise' are in reality a lesson of caution.
The superior man emblemed here by the 'yellow' and correct colour, is possessed of comprehension and discrimination. He occupies the correct position of supremacy, but that emblem is on the lower part of his person. His excellence is in the centre of his being, but it diffuses a complacency over his four limbs, and is manifested in his conduct of affairs:— this is the perfection of excellence. The subject of the Yin or divided line thinking himself equal to the subject of the yang, or undivided line, there is sure to be 'a contest.' As if indignant at there being no acknowledgment of the superiority of the subject of the yang line, the text uses the term 'dragons.' But still the subject of neither line can leave his class, and hence we have 'the blood' mentioned. The mention of that as being both 'azure and yellow' indicates the mixture of heaven and earth. Heaven's colour is azure and earth's is yellow.

雷水 ䷂ 屯 ③

屯、元亨、利貞、勿用有攸往、利建侯。

象曰、屯、剛柔始交而難生、動乎險中、大亨貞。雷雨之動、滿盈、天造草昧、宜建侯、而不寧。

象曰、雲雷屯、君子以、經綸。

初九、磐桓、利居貞、利建侯。象曰、雖磐桓、志行正也、以貴下賤、大得民也。

六二、屯如邅如。乘馬班如、匪寇、婚媾、女子貞不字、十年、乃字。象曰、六二之難、乘剛也、十年乃字、反常也。

六三、卽鹿无虞、惟入于林中、君子幾、不如舍、往、吝。象曰、卽鹿无虞、以從禽也、君子舍之、往、吝窮也。

六四、乘馬班如、求婚媾、往、吉、无不利。象曰、求而往、明也。

九五、屯其膏。小貞、吉、大貞、凶。象曰、屯其膏、施未光也。

上六、乘馬班如、泣血漣如。象曰、泣血漣如、何可長也?

둔屯은 크게 형통하고, 곧음이 이로우니 가는 바를 두지 말고 제후를 세움이 이롭다.

초9는 나아가지 못하니, 바른 데에 거하는 것이 이로우며 제후를 세움이 이롭다.

62는 어려운 듯 머뭇거리며 말을 타고 맴도니, 도적이 아니면 혼인하리니 여자가 곧아서 시집가지 않다가 십년 뒤에야 시집간다.

63은 사슴사냥을 나가도 몰이하는 사람이 없다. 오직 숲속으로 들어가기만 하니, 군자는 조짐을 보아 그만두는 것만 못하다. 그만두지 않고 그대로 가면 궁색하게 될 것이다.

64는 말을 타고 머뭇거렸으나 혼인을 구해서 가면 길하여 이롭지 않음이 없다.

95는 은택을 펴기 어려우니, 작은 일은 곧으면 길하지만, 큰 일은 곧아도 흉할 것이다.

상6은 말을 탔다가 내려서 피눈물이 흐른다.

Tun indicates that in the case which it presupposes there will be great progress and success, and the advantage will come from being correct and firm. But any movement in advance should not be lightly undertaken. There will be advantage in appointing feudal princes.

1. F9, undivided, shows the difficulty its subject has in advancing. It will be advantageous for him to abide correct and firm; advantageous also to be made a feudal ruler.
2. 62, divided, shows its subject distressed and obliged to re-turn; even the horses of her chariot also seem to be retreating. But not by a spoiler is she assailed, but by one who seeks her to be his wife. The young lady maintains her firm correctness, and declines a union. After ten years she will be united, and have children.
3. 63, divided, shows one following the deer without the guidance of the forester, and only finding himself in the midst of the forest. The superior man, acquainted with the secret risks, think it better to give up the chase. If he went forward, he would regret it.
4. 64, divided, shows its subject as a lady, the horses of whose chariot appear in retreat. She seeks, however, the help of him who seeks her to be his wife. Advance will be fortunate; all will turn out advantageously.
5. 95, undivided, shows the difficulties in the way of its sub-ject's dispensing the rich favours that might be expected from him. With firm-ness and correctness there will be good fortune in small things; even with them in great things there will be evil.
6. L6, divided, shows its subject with the horses of his cha-riot obliged to retreat, and weeping tears of blood in streams.

水山 ䷃ 蒙 (四)

蒙、亨。匪我求童蒙、童蒙、求我、初筮、告、再三、瀆、瀆則不告。利貞。

彖曰、蒙、山下有險、險而止、蒙。蒙亨、以亨行、時中也。匪我求童蒙、童蒙求我、志應也。初筮告、以剛中也、再三瀆瀆則不告、瀆蒙也。蒙以養正、聖功也。

象曰、山下出泉、蒙、君子以、果行、育德。

初六、發蒙、利用刑人、用說桎梏、以往、吝。象曰、利用刑人、以正法也。

九二、包蒙、吉。納婦、吉、子克家。象曰、子克家、剛柔接也。

六三、勿用取女、見金夫、不有躬、无攸利。象曰、勿用取女、行、不順也。

六四、困蒙、吝。象曰、困蒙之吝、獨遠實也。

六五、童蒙、吉。象曰、童蒙之吉、順以巽也。

上九、擊蒙、不利爲寇、利禦寇。象曰、利用禦寇、上下順也。

몽蒙은 형통한 것이니 내가 몽매한 어린아이를 구하는 것이 아니라, 몽매한 어린아이가 나를 찾는 것이다. 처음 점치거든 알리고 두 번, 세 번하면 어지럽혀진다. 어지럽혀지면 알리지 않으니 곧게 함이 이롭다.

초6은 몽매蒙昧함을 일깨움에 형벌을 이용하되, 그 뒤로 형틀을 벗겨 주는 것이 이롭고, 그대로 행하면 궁색할 것이다.
92는 몽매한 자를 두루 감싸면 길하고, 또 아내를 맞으면 길하니, 아들이 집안을 다스릴 것이다.
63은 여자를 취하지 않는 것이니, 돈 많은 남자를 보고 몸을 두지 않으면 이로움이 없을 것이다.
64는 곤궁하고 몽매하니 궁색하다.
65는 어린아이의 몽매함이니 길하다.
상9는 몽매한 것을 일깨워 주는 것이니, 도적이 되는 것은 이롭지 않지만, 도적을 막는 것은 이롭다.

Meng indicates that in the case witch it presupposes there will be progress and success. I do not go and seek the youthful and inexperienced, but he comes and seeks me. When he shows the sincerity that marks the first recourse to divination, I instruct him. if he apply a second and third time, that is troublesome; and I do not instruct the troublesome. there will be advantage in being firm and correct.

1. F6, divided, has respect to the dispelling of ignorance. It will be advantageous to us punishment for that purpose, and to remove the shackles from the mind. But going on in that way of punishment will give occasion for regret.
2. 92, undivided, shows its subject exercising forbearance with the ignorant, in which there will be good fortune; and admitting even the goodness of women, which will also be fortunate. He may be described also as a son able to sustain the burden of his family.
3. 63, divided, seem to say that one should not marry a woman whose emblem it might be, for that, when she sees a man of wealth, she will not keep her person from him, and in no wise will advantage come from her.
4. 64, divided, shows its subject as if bound in chains of ignorance. There will be occasion for regret.
5. 65, divided, shows its subject as a simple lad without experience. There will be good fortune.
6. L9, undivided, we see one smiting the ignorant youth. But no advantage will come from doing him an injury. Advantage would com from warding off injury from him.

天水 ䷄ 需 ⑤

需、有孚、光亨、貞吉、利涉大川。

彖曰、需、須也、險、在前也、剛健而不陷、其義不困窮矣、需有孚光亨貞吉、位乎天位、以正中也。利涉大川、往有功也。

象曰、雲上于天、需、君子以、飲食宴樂。

初九、需于郊、利用恒、无咎。象曰、需于郊、不犯難行也、利用恒无咎、未失常也。

九二、需于沙、小有言、終吉。象曰、需于沙、衍、在中也、雖小有言、以吉、終也。

九三、需于泥、致寇至。象曰、需于泥、災在外也、白我致寇、敬愼、不敗也。

六四、需于血、出自穴。象曰、需于血、順以聽也。

九五、需于酒食、貞、吉。象曰、酒食貞吉、以中正也。

上六、入于穴、有不速之客三人、來、敬之、終吉。象曰、不速之客來敬之終吉、雖不當位、未大失也。

수需는 믿음이 있어서 빛나고 형통하고 곧고 길하니, 큰 내를 건넘이 이롭다.

초9는 들에서 기다림이니, 항상함을 씀이 이롭고 허물이 없다.
92는 모래밭에서 기다림이니, 조금 말이 있으나 마침내 길할 것이다.
93은 진흙 속에서 기다림이니, 도둑이 이르게 된다.
64는 피에서 기다리다가 함정에서 빠져나간다.
95는 술과 음식에서 기다림이니, 곧고 길하다.
상6은 구멍으로 들어가는 것이다. 청하지도 않은 손님 세 사람이 올 것이니, 공경하면 마침내 길할 것이다.

Xu intimates that, with the sincerity which is declared in it, there will be brilliant success. With firmness there will be good fortune; and it will be advantageous to cross the great stream.

1. F9, undivided, shows its subject waiting in the distant border. It will be well for him constantly to maintain the purpose thus shown, in which case there will be no error.
2. 92, undivided, shows its subject waiting on the sand of the mountain stream. He will suffer the small injury of being spoken against, but in the end there will be good fortune.
3. 93, undivided, shows its subject in the mud close by the stream. He thereby invites the approach of injury.
4. 94, divided, shows its subject waiting in the place of blood. But he will get out of the cavern.
5. 95, undivided, shows its subject waiting amidst the appliances of a feast. Though his firmness and correctness there will be good fortune.
6. L6, divided, shows its subject entered into the cavern. But there are three guests coming, without being urged, to his help. If he receive them respectfully, there will be good fortune in the end.

水天 ䷅ 訟 ⑥

訟、有孚窒、惕、中、吉、終、凶、利見大人、不利涉大川。

象曰、訟、上剛下險、險而健、訟。訟有孚窒惕、中吉、剛來而得中也。終凶、訟不可成也。利見大人、尚中正也。不利涉大川、入于淵也。

象曰、天與水違行、訟、君子以、作事謀始。

初六、不永所事、小有言、終吉。象曰、不永所事、訟不可長也、雖小有言、其辯、明也。

九二、不克訟、歸而逋、其邑人、三百戶、无眚。象曰、不克訟、歸逋竄也、自下訟上、患至掇也。

六三、食舊德、貞、厲、終吉、或從王事、无成。象曰、食舊德、從上、吉也。

九四、不克訟、復卽命、渝、安貞、吉。象曰、復卽命渝安貞、不失也。

九五、訟、元吉。象曰、訟元吉、以中正也。

上九、或錫之鞶帶、終朝三褫之。象曰、以訟受服、亦不足敬也。

송訟은 믿음이 있으나 막혀서 두려우니, 중간은 길하고 끝은 흉하니요, 대인大人을 만나면 이롭고, 위험하게 큰내를 건너는 것은 이롭지 않다.

초6은 송사訟事를 길게 끌지 않으면 조금 말이 있어도 마침내 길할 것이다.

92는 송사에서 이기지 못하니, 돌아가 도망해서 그 읍의 사람이 삼백호이면 재앙이 없을 것이다.

63은 옛 덕을 먹고 살며 곧게 하면 위태롭지만 결국은 길할 것이니, 혹 왕의 일을 하더라도 이룸은 없을 것이다.

94는 송사에 이기지 못하니, 본성에 회복하여 마음을 바꿔 편안하고 곧으면 길할 것이다.

95는 송사에 크게 길할 것이다.

상9는 혹 허리띠를 상으로 하사하더라도, 아침이 지날 때까지 세 번 빼앗길 것이다.

Song intimates how, though there is sincerity in one's contention, he will yet meet with opposition and obstruction: but if he cherish an apprehensive caution, there will be good fortune, while, if he must prosecute the contention to the bitter end, there will be evil. It will be advantageous to see the great man: it will not be advantageous to cross the great stream.

1. F6, divided, shows its subject not perpetuating the matter about which the contention is. He will suffer the small injury of being spoken against, but the end will be fortunate.
2. 92, undivided, shows its subject unequal to the contention. If he retire and keep concealed where the inhabitants of his city are only three hundred families, he will fall into no mistake.
3. 63, divided, shows its subject keeping in the old place assigned for his support, and firmly correct. Perilous as the position is, there will be good fortune in the end. Should he perchance engage in the king's business, he will not claim the merit of achievement.
4. 94, undivided, shows its subject unequal to the contention. He returns to the study of heaven's ordinances, changes his wish to contend, and rests in being firm and correct. There will be good fortune.
5. 95, undivided, shows its subject contending;-and with great good fortune.
6. L9, undivided, shows how its subject may have the leathern belt conferred on him by the sovereign, and thrice it shall be taken from him in a morning.

水地 ䷆ 師 ⑦

師、貞、丈人吉、无咎。

象曰、師、衆也、貞、正也。能以衆正、可以王矣。剛中而應、行險而順、以此毒天下而民、從之、吉又何咎矣！

象曰、地中有水師、君子以、容民畜衆。

初六、師出以律、否、臧、凶。象曰、師出以律、失律、凶也。

九二、在師、中、吉、无咎、王三錫命。象曰、在師中吉、承天寵也、王三錫命、懷萬邦也。

六三、師或輿尸、凶。象曰、師或輿尸、大无功也。

六四、師左次、无咎。象曰、左次无咎、未失常也。

六五、田有禽、利執言、无咎、長子帥師、弟子輿尸、貞、凶。象曰、長子帥師、以中行也、弟子輿尸、使不當也。

上六、大君、有命、開國承家、小人勿用。象曰、大君有命、以正功也、小人勿用、必亂邦也。

사師는 바르게 하는 것이니, 장인丈人이라야 길하고 허물이 없을 것이다.

초6은 군사가 나아가는데 군율로써 하는 것이니, 그렇지 않으면 착하더라도 흉하다.
92는 군대에서 중도中道로써 처리해야 길하고 허물이 없다. 왕이 세 번 명을 내린다.
63은 군사가 혹 시체를 수레에 싣게 되니, 흉할 것이다.
64는 군사가 작전상 후퇴하는 것이니, 허물이 없을 것이다.
65는 밭에 새가 있으면 잡는 것이 이로우니, 허물이 없을 것이다. 큰 아들이 군사를 거느리고, 작은 아들은 시체를 실으니, 곧더라도 흉할 것이다.
상6은 대군大君이 명령하니, 나라를 열고 가읍家邑을 계승함에 소인小人은 쓰지 말 것이다.

Shi indicates how, in the case which it supposes, with firmness and correctness, and a leader of age and experience, there will be good fortune and no error.

1. F6, divided, shows the host going forth according to the rules for such a movement. If these be not good, there will be evil.
2. 92, undivided, shows the leader in the midst of the host. There will be good for- tune and no error. The king has thrice conveyed to him the orders of his favour.
3. 63, divided, shows how the host may, possibly, have many inefficient leaders. There will be evil.
4. 64, divided, shows the host in retreat. There is no error.
5. 65, divided, shows birds in the fields, which it will be ad- vantageous to seize and destroy. In that case there will be no error. If the oldest son leads the host, and younger men idly occupy offices assigned to them, however firm and correct he may be, there will be evil.
6. L6, divided, shows the great ruler delivering his charges, appointing some to be rulers of states, and others to un- dertake the head- ship of clans; but small men should not be employed in such positions.

地水 比 (八)

比、吉、原筮、元永貞、无咎。不寧、方來、後、夫、凶。

象曰、比、吉也、比、輔也、下順從也。原筮元永貞无咎、以剛中也。不寧方來、上下應也。後夫凶、其道窮也。

象曰、地上有水、比、先王、以、建萬國、親諸侯。

初六、有孚比之、无咎、有孚盈缶、終、來有他吉。象曰、比之初六、有他吉也。

六二、比之自內、貞、吉。象曰、比之自內、不自失也。

六三、比之匪人。象曰、比之匪人、不亦傷乎？

六四、外比之、貞、吉。象曰、外比於賢、以從上也。

九五、顯比、王用三驅、失前禽、邑人不誡、吉。象曰、顯比之吉、位正中也、舍逆取順、失前禽也、邑人不誡、上使中也。

上六、比之无首、凶。象曰、比之无首、无所終也。

비比는 길한 것이니 점을 살펴보건대 으뜸이 되는 이가 길이 곧아야 허물이 없을 것이다. 편치 않은 것이 찾아오니, 뒤처지는 자는 흉할 것이다.

초6은 믿음을 두어 친해야 허물이 없을 것이니, 믿음을 둠이 질그릇에 가득하면 마침내 다른 길함이 있을 것이다.
62는 친한 것을 안으로부터 하니 바르고 길하다.
63은 친할만한 사람이 아니다.
64는 밖으로 친하니 바르게 하여 길하다.
95는 친함을 드러내니, 왕이 세 군데로 몰며 사냥할 때 앞으로 향하는 짐승을 잡지 않으며, 읍 사람이 경계하지 않으니 길하다.
상6은 친해도 시작이 없으니 흉하다.

Bi indicates that under the conditions which it supposes there is good fortune. But let the prin-cipal party intended in it re-examine himself, as if by divination, whether his virtue be great, uninter-mitting, and firm. If it be so, there will be no error. Those who have not rest will then come to him; and with those who are too late in coming it will be ill.

1. F6, divided, shows its subject seek-ing by his sincerity to win the attachment of his object. There will be no error. Let the breast be full of sincerity as an earthenware vessel is of its contents, and it will in the end bring other advantages.
2. 62, divided, we see the movement towards union and at-tachment proceeding from the inward mind. With firm cor-rectness there will be good fortune.
3. 63, divided, we see its subject seeking for union with such as ought not to be associated with.
4. 64, divided, we see its subject seeking for union with the one beyond himself. With firm correctness there will be good fortune.
5. 95, undivided, affords the most illustrious instance of seek-ing union and attachment. We seem to see in it the king urging his pursuit of the game only in three directions, and allowing the escape of all the animals before him, while the people of his towns do not warn one another to pre-vent it. There will be good fortune.
6. L6, divided, we see one seeking union and attachment without having taken the first step to such an end. There will be evil.

天風 ☴☰ 小畜 ⑨

小畜、亨、密雲不雨、自我西郊。

彖曰、小畜、柔得位而上下應之、曰小畜。健而巽、剛中而志行、乃亨。密雲不雨、尚往也、自我西郊、施未行也。

象曰、風行天上、小畜、君子以、懿文德。

初九、復、自道、何其咎、吉。象曰、復自道、其義吉也。

九二、牽復、吉。象曰、牽復、在中、亦不自失也。

九三、輿說(脫)輻、夫妻反目。象曰、夫妻反目、不能正室也。

六四、有孚、血去、惕出、无咎。象曰、有孚惕出、上合志也。

九五、有孚、攣如、富以其鄰。象曰、有孚攣如、不獨富也。

上九、旣雨旣處、尚德、載、婦貞、厲、月幾望、君子征、凶。

象曰、旣雨旣處、德、積載也、君子征凶、有所疑也。

소축小畜은 형통한 것이니, 구름은 짙으나 비는 내리지 않고, 서쪽 교외로부터 일어난다.

초9는 제 길로 돌아오니, 무슨 허물이 있겠는가? 길할 것이다.
92는 이끌어서 회복하는 것이니, 길할 것이다.
93은 수레의 바퀴가 빠지는 것이니, 남편과 아내가 반목反目한다.
64는 믿음을 두면 피를 흘리지 않고 두려움에서 벗어나 허물이 없을 것이다.
95는 믿음을 가지고 있는지라 끌어당겨서 부유함을 그 이웃과 함께 한다.
상9는 이미 비가 오고, 그치는 것은 덕을 숭상하여 가득 차게 한 것이니, 지어미가 곧게만 하면 위태로울 것이다. 달이 거의 보름이니, 군자가 가면 흉할 것이다.

Xiaochu indicates that under its conditions there will be progress and success. We see dense clouds, but no rain coming from our borders in the west.

1. F9, undivided, shows its subject returning and pursuing his own course. What mistake should he fall into? There will be good fortune.
2. 92, undivided, shows its subject, by the attraction of the former line, returning to the proper course. There will be good fortune.
3. 93, undivided, suggests the idea of a carriage, the strap beneath which has been removed, or of a husband and wife looking on each other with averted eyes.
4. 64, divided, shows its subject possessed of sincerity. The danger of bloodshed is thereby averted, and his ground for apprehension dismissed. There will be no mistake.
5. 95, undivided, shows its subject possessed of sincerity, and drawing others to unite with him. Rich in resources, he employs his neighbours in the same cause with himself.
6. L9, undivided, shows how the rain has fallen, and the onward progress is stayed;-so must we value the full accumulation of the virtue represented by the upper trigram. But a wife exercising restraint, however firm and correct she may be, is in a position of peril, and like the moon approaching to the full. If the superior man prosecute his measures in such circumstances, there will be evil.

澤天 履 ⑩

履 履虎尾、不咥人、亨。

象曰、履、柔履剛也、說而應乎乾、是以履虎尾不咥人亨。剛中正、履帝位、而不疚、光明也。

象曰、上天下澤、履、君子以、辯上下、定民志。

初九、素履、往、无咎。象曰、素履之往、獨行願也。

九二、履道坦坦、幽人、貞、吉。象曰、幽人貞吉、中不自亂也。

六三、眇能視、跛能履、履虎尾、咥人、凶、武人、爲于大君。象曰、眇能視、不足以有明也、跛能履、不足以與行也、咥人之凶、位不當也、武人爲於大君、志剛也。

九四、履虎尾、愬愬、終吉。象曰、愬愬終吉、志行也。

九五、夬履、貞、厲。象曰、夬履貞厲、位正當也。

上九、視履、考祥、其旋、元吉。象曰、元吉在上、大有慶也。

호랑이 꼬리를 밟더라도 사람을 물지 않으니, 형통할 것이다.

초9는 소박하게 밟아 가면 허물이 없을 것이다.

92는 밟는 길이 탄탄하니, 세속을 떠난 사람이 곧게하여 길할 것이다.

63은 소경이 보고 절름발이가 걷는 것이다. 호랑이 꼬리를 밟아서 사람을 무니 흉하다. 무인武人이 대군大君이 된다.

94는 호랑이 꼬리를 밟으나, 조심하고 조심하면 마침내 길할 것이다.

95는 결단해서 밟아나가는 것이니, 바르게 하더라도 위태로울 것이다.

상9는 그 밟아온 것을 보고 그 상서로운 것을 살피되, 되돌리면 크게 길할 것이다.

Lu suggests the idea of one treading on the tail of a tiger, which does not bite him. There will be progress and success.

1. F9, undivided, shows its subject treading his accustomed path. If he go forward, there will be no error.
2. 92, undivided, shows its subject treading the path that is level and easy;- a quiet and solitary man, to whom, if he be firm and correct, there will be good fortune.
3. 63, divided, shows a one-eyed man who thinks he can see; a lame man who thinks he can walk well; one who treads on the tail of a tiger and is bitten. All this indicates ill fortune. We have a mere bravo acting the part of a great ruler.
4. 94, undivided, shows its subject treading on the tail of a tiger. He becomes full of apprehensive caution, and in the end there will be good fortune.
5. 95, undivided, shows the resolute tread of its subject. Though he be firm and correct, there will be peril.
6. L9, undivided, tells us to look at the whole course that is trodden, and examine the presage which that gives. If it be complete and without failure, there will be great good fortune.

天地 ䷊ 泰 (十一)

泰、小往 大來、吉、亨。

彖曰、泰小往大來吉亨。則是天地交而萬物、通也、上下交而其志同也。內陽而外陰、內健而外順、內君子而外小人、君子道長、小人道消也。

象曰、天地交泰、后以、財成天地之道、輔相天地之宜、以左右民。

初九、拔茅茹、以其彙、征、吉。象曰、拔茅征吉、志在外也。

九二、包荒、用馮河、不遐遺、朋亡、得尚于中行。象曰、包荒得尚于中行、以光大也。

九三、无平不陂、无往不復、艱貞、无咎、勿恤、其孚、于食、有福。象曰、无往不復、天地際也。

六四、翩翩、不富以其鄰、不戒以孚。象曰、翩翩不富、皆失實也、不戒以孚、中心願也。

六五、帝乙歸妹、以祉、元吉。象曰、以祉元吉、中以行願也。

上六、城復于隍、勿用師、自邑告命、貞、吝。象曰、城復于隍、其命、亂也。

태泰는 작은 것이 가고 큰 것이 오니 형통할 것이다.

초9는 띠의 뿌리를 뽑는 것이다. 그 무리를 지어서 가니 길할 것이다.

92는 거친 것을 포용하고 과감하게 강을 건너며, 먼 것도 버리지 아니하며 붕당朋黨이 없으면 중도中道로 가는 것이 잘 맞을 것이다.

93은 평탄한 것은 기울어지며, 나간 것은 반드시 돌아오니, 어려워도 곧게 하면 허물이 없을 것이다. 근심하지 않아도 성실함이 있으니, 식록食祿에 복이 있을 것이다.

64는 훨훨 나는 듯이 부유하지 않아도 그 이웃과 함께하니, 경계하지 않아도 믿을 수 있다.

65는 제을帝乙이 누이동생을 시집보내니, 복을 받고 크게 길할 것이다.

상6은 성城이 터로 돌아감이니, 무력武力으로 싸우지 말고 살고 있는 읍邑에서 명령을 세워야 하니, 바르게 해도 궁색할 것이다.

In *Tai* we see the little gone and the great come. It indicates that there will be good fortune, with progress and success.

1. F9, undivided, suggests the idea of grass pulled up, and bringing with it other stalks with whose roots it is connected. Advance on the part of its subject will be fortunate.
2. 92, undivided, shows one who can bear with the uncultivated, will cross the Ho without a boat, does not forget the distant, and has no selfish friendships. Thus does he prove himself acting in accordance with the course of the due Mean.
3. 93, undivided, shows that, while there is no state of peace that is not liable to be disturbed, and no departure of evil men so that they shall not return, yet when one is firm and correct, as he realises the distresses that may arise, he will commit no error. There is no occasion for sadness at the certainty of such recurring changes; and in this mood the happiness of the present may be long enjoyed.
4. 64, divided, shows its subject fluttering down;-not relying on his own rich resources, but calling in his neighbours. They all come not as having received warning, but in the sincerity of their hearts.
5. 65, divided, reminds us of king ti-yi's rule about the marriage of his younger sister. By such a course there is happiness and there will be great good fortune.
6. L6, divided, shows us the city wall returned into the moat. It is not the time to use the army. The subject of the line may, indeed, announce his orders to the people of his own city; but however correct and firm he may be, he will have cause for regret.

地天 ䷋ 否 (十二)

否 否之匪人、不利君子貞、大往小來。

象曰、否之匪人、不利君子貞、大往小來。則是天地不交而萬物、不通也、上下不交而天下无邦也。內陰而外陽、內柔而外剛、內小人而外君子、小人道長、君子道消也。

象曰、天地不交否、君子以、儉德辟難、不可榮以祿。

初六、拔茅茹、以其彙、貞、吉、亨。象曰、拔茅貞吉、志在君也。

六二、包承、小人、吉、大人、否、亨。象曰、大人否亨、不亂羣也。

六三、包羞。象曰、包羞、位不當也。

九四、有命、无咎、疇離祉。象曰、有命无咎、志行也。

九五、休否、大人、吉、其亡其亡、繫于苞桑。象曰、大人之吉、位正當也。

上九、傾否、先否、後喜。象曰、否終則傾、何可長也。

비否는 사람이 아니니, 군자의 곧음이 이롭지 못하다. 큰 것이 가고 작은 것이 온다.

초6은 띠 뿌리를 뽑으니 얽혀 있다. 그 무리로써 함이니, 곧으면 길해서 형통할 것이다.

62는 감싸고 받드니 소인小人은 길하고 대인大人은 막히나 형통할 것이다.

63은 부끄러운 마음을 감싸 안았다.

94는 명을 내리면 허물이 없어서, 동료가 복을 받을 것이다.

95는 막힘을 그치게 한다. 대인大人의 길함이니 망할까 조심해야만 뽕나무에 맬 수 있다.

상9는 막힌 것이 기울어짐이니, 먼저는 막히고 뒤에는 기쁘다.

In *Fou* there is the want of good understanding between the different classes of men, and its indication is unfavourable to the firm and correct course of the superior man. We see in it the great gone and the little come.

1. F6, divided, suggests the idea of grass pulled up, and bringing with it other stalks with whose roots it is connected. With firm correctness on the part of its subject, there will bc good fortune and progress.
2. 62, divided, shows its subject patient and obedient. To the small man comporting himself so there will be good fortune. If the great man comport himself as the distress and obstruction require, he will have success.
3. 63, divided, shows its subject ashamed of the purpose folded in his breast.
4. 94, undivided, shows its subject acting in accordance with the ordination of Heaven, and committing no error. His companions will come and share in his happiness.
5. 95, undivided, we see him who brings the distress and obstruction to a close,-the great man and fortunate. But let him say, 'We may perish! We may perish!' so shall the state of things become firm, as if bound to a clump of bushy mulberry trees.
6. L9, undivided, shows the overthrow and removal of the condition of distress and obstruction. Before this there was that condition. hereafter there will be joy.

天火 ䷌ 同人 ⑬

同人　同人于野、亨、利涉大川、利君子、貞。

彖曰、同人、柔得位、得中而應乎乾、曰同人。同人曰同人于野亨利涉大川、乾行也。文明以健、中正而應、君子正也。唯君子、爲能通天下之志。

象曰、天與火同人、君子以、類族、辨物。

初九、同人于門、无咎。象曰、出門同人、又誰咎也！

六二、同人于宗、吝。象曰、同人于宗、吝道也。

九三、伏戎于莽、升其高陵、三歲不興。象曰、伏戎于莽、敵剛也、三歲不興、安行也？

九四、乘其墉、弗克攻、吉。象曰、乘其墉、義弗克也、其吉、則困而反則也。

九五、同人、先號咷而後笑、大師克、相遇。象曰、同人之先、以中直也、大師相遇、言相克也。

上九、同人于郊、无悔。象曰、同人于郊、志未得也。

들에서 사람과 같이 하면 형통할 것이니, 큰 내를 거느는 것이 이로우며, 군자의 바름이 이롭다.

초9는 문밖에서 사람을 만나는 것이니, 허물이 없을 것이다.

62는 종족끼리 만나는 것이니, 궁색하다.

93은 군사를 숲에 잠복시키고 높은 언덕에 올라서 삼년을 일어나지 못한다.

94는 그 담 위에 오르되 공격하지 못하니, 길할 것이다.

95는 사람을 만나서 먼저는 부르고 울부짖다가 뒤에는 웃으니, 큰 군사로 이겨야 서로 만날 것이다.

상9는 교외에서 사람들을 만나니, 후회가 없다.

Tongren or 'Union of men' appears here as we find it in the remote districts of the country, indicating progress and success. It will be advantageous to cross the great stream. It will be advantageous to maintain the firm correctness of the superior man.

1. F9, undivided, shows the representative of the union of men just issuing from his gate. There will be no error.
2. 62, divided, shows the representative of the union of men in relation with his kindred. There will be occasion for regret.
3. 93, undivided, shows its subject with his arms hidden in the thick grass, and at the top of a high mound. But for three years he makes no demonstration.
4. 94, undivided, shows its subject mounted on the city wall; but he does not proceed to make the attack he contemplate. tThere will be good fortune.
5. 95, undivided, the representative of the union of the union of men first wails and cries out, and then laughs, His great host conquers, and he and the subject of the second line meet together.
6. L9, undivided, shows the representative of the union of men in the suburbs. There will be no occasion for repentance.

火天 大有 ☲☰ 十四

大有、元亨。

彖曰、大有、柔得尊位、大中而上下應之、曰大有。其德、剛健而文明、應乎天而時行、是以元亨。

象曰、火在天上、大有、君子以、遏惡揚善、順天休命。

初九、无交害、匪咎、艱則无咎。象曰、大有初九、无交害也。

九二、大車以載、有攸往、无咎。象曰、大車以載、積中不敗也。

九三、公用亨于天子、小人、弗克。象曰、公用亨于天子、小人、害也。

九四、匪其彭、无咎。象曰、匪其彭无咎、明辯晳也。

六五、厥孚交如、威如、吉。象曰、厥孚交如、信以發志也、威如之吉、易而无備也。

上九、自天祐之、吉无不利。象曰、大有上吉、自天祐也。

대유大有는 크게 형통하니라.

초9는 사귐에 해가 없으니 허물이 아니지만, 어렵게 하면 허물이 없을 것이다.
92는 큰 수레로써 싣는 것이니, 가는 바가 있으면 허물이 없을 것이다.
93은 공公이 천자天子에게 바치는 것이니, 소인小人은 감당하지 못할 것이다.
94는 위세를 부리지 않으면 허물이 없을 것이다.
65는 믿음으로 사귀는 것이니, 위엄이 있어서 길하다.
상9는 하늘로부터 돕는 것이니, 길하여 이롭지 않음이 없다.

Tayou indicates that, under the circumstances which it implies, there will be great progress and success.

1. F9, undivided, there is no approach to what is injurious, and there is no error. Let there be a realisation of the difficulty and danger of the position, and there will be no error to the end.
2. 92, undivided, we have a large waggon with its load. In whatever direction advance is made, there will be no error.
3. 93, undivided, shows us a feudal prince presenting his offerings to the Son of Heaven. A small man would be unequal to such a duty.
4. 94, undivided, shows its subject keeping his great resources under restraint. There will be no error.
5. 65, divided, shows the sincerity of its subject reciprocated by that of all the others represented in the hexagram. Let him display a proper majesty, and there will be good fortune.
6. L9, undivided, shows its subject with help accorded to him from Heaven. There will be good fortune, advantage in every respect.

山地 ䷎ 謙 ⑮

謙、亨、君子有終。

象曰、謙亨。天道下濟而光明、地道卑而上行。天道、虧盈而益謙、地道、變盈而流謙、鬼神、害盈而福謙、人道、惡盈而好謙。謙、尊而光、卑而不可踰、君子之終也。

象曰、地中有山、謙、君子以、裒多益寡、稱物平施。

初六、謙謙君子、用涉大川、吉。象曰、謙謙君子、卑以自牧也。

六二、鳴謙、貞、吉。象曰、鳴謙貞吉、中心得也。

九三、勞謙、君子有終、吉。象曰、勞謙君子、萬民、服也。

六四、无不利撝謙。象曰、无不利撝謙、不違則也。

六五、不富以其鄰、利用侵伐、无不利。象曰、利用侵伐、征不服也。

上六、鳴謙、利用行師、征邑國。象曰、鳴謙、志未得也、可用行師、征邑國也。

겸謙은 형통한 것이니 군자에게 제대로 된 마침이 있다.

초6은 겸손하고 또 겸손한 군자이니, 큰 내를 건너더라도 길할 것이다.
62는 겸손을 떨치니, 바르고 길할 것이다.
93은 겸손에 힘쓰니, 군자에게 마침이 있어 길할 것이다.
64는 겸손을 발휘하니, 이롭지 않음이 없다.
65는 부유하지 않아도 이웃과 함께 하며, 정벌하는 것이 이롭지 아니 함이 없다.
상6은 겸손을 떨치니, 군사를 동원해서 읍국邑國을 치는 것이 이롭다.

Qian indicates progress and success. The superior man, being humble as it implies, will have a good issue to his undertakings.

1. F6, divided, shows us the superior man who adds humility to humility. Even the great stream may be crossed with this, and there will be good fortune.
2. 62, divided, shows us humility that has made itself recognised. With firm correctness there will be good fortune.
3. 93, undivided, shows the superior man of acknowledged merit. He will maintain his success to the end, and have good fortune.
4. 64, divided, shows one, whose action would be in every way advantageous, stirring up the more his humility.
5. 65, divided, shows one who, without being rich, is able to employ his neighbours. He may advantageously use the force of arms. All his movements will be advantageous.
6. L6, divided, shows us humility that has made itself recognised. The subject of it will with advantage put his hosts in motion; but he will only punish his own towns and state.

地雷 ䷏ 豫 (十六)

豫、利建侯行師。

象曰、豫、剛應而志行、順以動、豫。豫順以動故、天地、如之、而況建侯行師乎。天地以順動、故、日月、不過而四時不忒、聖人、以順動、則刑罰、清而民、服。豫之時義大矣哉。

象曰、雷出地奮、豫、先王、以、作樂崇德、殷薦之上帝、以配祖考。

初六、鳴豫、凶。象曰、初六鳴豫、志窮、凶也。

六二、介于石、不終日、貞、吉。象曰、不終日貞吉、以中正也。

六三、盱豫、悔、遲、有悔。象曰、盱豫有悔、位不當也。

九四、由豫、大有得、勿疑、朋、盍簪。象曰、由豫大有得、志大行也。

六五、貞、疾、恒不死。象曰、六五貞疾、乘剛也、恒不死、中未亡也。

上六、冥豫成、有渝、无咎。象曰、冥豫在上、何可長也。

예豫는 제후를 세우고 군사를 움직이는 것이 이롭다.

초6은 즐거움이 떨치니, 흉하다.
62는 절개가 돌같이 굳으니, 하루를 마칠 것도 없이 바르고 길하다.
63은 바라보며 즐거워하여 후회하며 늦어서 후회함이 있을 것이다.
94는 즐거움으로부터 말미암아 크게 얻으니, 의심하지 않으면 벗이 모여들 것이다.
65는 바르되 고질병을 얻었으나, 오랫동안 죽지 않을 것이다.
상6은 즐거움에 눈이 어두워지게 되었으나, 변함이 있으면 허물이 없을 것이다.

Yu indicates that, in the state which it implies, feudal princes may be set up, and the hosts put in motion, with advantage.

1. F6, divided, shows its subject proclaiming his pleasure and satisfection. There will be evil.
2. 62, divided, shows one who is firm as a rock. He sees a thing without waiting till it has come to pass ; with his firm correctness there will be good fortune.
3. 63, divided, shows one looking up for favours, while he indulges the feeling of pleasure and satisfaction. If he would understand! - If he be late in doing so, there will indeed be occasion for repentance.
4. 94, undivided, shows him from whom the harmony and satisfaction come. Great is the success which he obtains. Let him not allow suspicions to enter his mind, and thus friends will gather around him.
5. 65, divided, shows one with a chronic complaint, but who lives on without dying.
6. L6, divided, shows its subject with darkened mind devoted to the pleasure and satisfaction of the time; but if he change his course even when it may be considered as completed, there will be no error.

雷澤 ䷐ 隨 ⑰

隨、元亨、利貞、无咎。

彖曰、隨、剛來而不柔、動而說。隨、大亨、貞、无咎、而天下隨時。隨時之義大矣哉！

象曰、澤中有雷、隨、君子以、嚮晦入宴息。

初九、官有渝、貞、吉、出門交、有功。象曰、官有渝、從正、吉也、出門交有功、不失也。

六二、係小子、失丈夫。象曰、係小子、弗兼與也。

六三、係丈夫、失小子、隨、有求、得、利居貞。象曰、係丈夫、志舍下也。

九四、隨、有獲、貞、凶、有孚、在道、以明、何咎！象曰、隨有獲、其義凶也、有孚在道、明功也。

九五、孚于嘉、吉。象曰、孚於嘉吉、位正中也。

上六、拘係之、乃從維之、王用亨于西山。象曰、拘係之、上窮也。

수隨는 크게 형통하니, 바르게 해야 이롭고 허물이 없을 것이다.

초9는 주관함에 변함이 있으니, 바르게 하면 길하고, 문에 나가서 사귀면 공功이 있을 것이다.

62는 소자小子에게 매여서 장부丈夫를 잃을 것이다.

63은 장부丈夫에 매여서 소자小子를 잃으니, 따름에 구하는 것이 있으면 얻을 것이나, 바른 데 있으면 도울 것이다.

94는 따름에 얻음이 있으면 바르더라도 흉하니, 믿음을 두고 도道를 지켜서 밝히면 무슨 허물이 있겠는가?

95는 아름다운데서 미더우니 길할 것이다.

상6은 붙잡아 매여서 이에 따르니, 왕이 서산을 소통시킬 것이다.

Sui indicates that under its conditions there will be great progress and success. But it will be advantageous to be firm and correct. There will then be no error.

1. F9, undivided, shows us one changing the object of his pursuit; but if he be firm and correct, there will be good fortune. Going beyond his own gate to find associates, he will achieve merit.
2. 62, divided, shows us one who cleaves to the little boy, and lets go the man of age and experience.
3. 63, divided, shows us one who cleaves to the man of age and experience, and lets go the little boy. Such following will get what get what it seeks; but it will be advantageous to adhere to what is firm and correct.
4. 94, undivided, shows us one followed and obtaining adherents. Though he be firm and correct, there will be evil. If he be sincere however in his course, and make that evident, into what error will he fall?
5. 95, undivided, shows us the ruler sincere in fostering all that is excellent. There will be good fortune.
6. L6, divided, shows us that sincerity firmly held and clung to, yea, and bound fast. We see the king with it presenting his offerings on the western mountain.

風山 ䷑ 蠱 (十八)

蠱、元亨、利涉大川、先甲三日、後甲三日。

彖曰、蠱、剛上而柔下、巽而止、蠱。蠱元亨、而天下治也。利涉大川、往有事也。先甲三日、後甲三日、終則有始、天行也。

象曰、山下有風、蠱、君子以、振民、育德。

初六、幹父之蠱、有子、考、无咎、厲、終吉。象曰、幹父之蠱、意承考也。

九二、幹母之蠱、不可貞。象曰、幹母之蠱、得中道也。

九三、幹父之蠱、小有悔、无大咎。象曰、幹父之蠱、終无咎也。

六四、裕父之蠱、往、見吝。象曰、裕父之蠱、往、未得也。

六五、幹父之蠱、用譽。象曰、幹父用譽、承以德也。

上九、不事王侯、高尚其事。象曰、不事王侯、志可則也。

고蠱는 크게 형통하여, 큰 내를 건너는 것이 이로우며, 법령에 앞서 사흘을 두며 법령의 뒤에 사흘을 둔다.

초6은 아비의 일을 맡는 것이니, 자식이 있으면 아비의 허물이 없을 것이니, 위태로우나 마침내 길할 것이다.
92는 어미의 일을 맡는 것이니, 바르게만 할 수 없을 것이다.
93은 아비의 일을 하니, 조금의 후회가 있으나 큰 허물은 없을 것이다.
64는 아비의 일을 여유롭게 처리하나, 그대로 가면 궁색해질 것이다.
65는 아비의 일을 하니, 명예를 얻을 것이다.
상9는 왕후王侯의 일을 하지 않고, 그 일을 높여 숭상한다.

Gu indicates great progress and success to him who deals properly with the condition represented by it. There will be advantage in efforts like that of crossing the great stream. He should weigh well, however, the events of three days before the turning point, and those to be done three days after it.

1. F6, divided, shows a son dealing with the troubles caused by his father. If he be an able son, the father will escape the blame of having erred. The position is perilous, but there will be good fortune in the end.
2. 92, undivided, shows a son dealing with the troubles caused by his mother. He should not carry his firm correctness to the utmost.
3. 93, undivided, shows a son dealing with the troubles caused by his father. There may be some small occasion for repentance, but there will not be any great error.
4. 64, divided, shows a son viewing indulgently the troubles caused by his father. If he go forward, he will find cause to regret it.
5. 65, divided, shows a son dealing with the troubles caused by his father. He obtains the praise of using the fit instrument for his work.
6. L9, undivided, shows us one who does not serve either king or feudal lord, but in a lofty spirit prefers to attend to his own affairs.

澤地 臨 ⑲

臨、元亨、利貞、至于八月、有凶。

彖曰、臨、剛浸而長、說而順、剛中而應。大亨以正、天之道也。至于八月有凶、消不久也。

象曰、澤上有地、臨、君子以、教思无窮、容保民、无疆。

初九、咸臨、貞、吉。象曰、咸臨貞吉、志行正也。

九二、咸臨、吉、无不利。象曰、咸臨吉无不利、未順命也。

六三、甘臨、无攸利、旣憂之、无咎。象曰、甘臨、位不當也、旣憂之、咎不長也。

六四、至臨、无咎。象曰、至臨无咎、位當也。

六五、知臨、大君之宜、吉。象曰、大君之宜、行中之謂也。

上六、敦臨、吉、无咎。象曰、敦臨之吉、志在內也。

임臨은 크게 형통하고 곧음이 이로우나, 팔월에 이르러 흉함이 있을 것이다.

초9는 감응해서 임하는 것이니, 바르게 하면 길할 것이다.
92는 감응해서 임하는 것이니, 길해서 이롭지 않음이 없다.
63은 달콤하게 임하여, 이로운 바가 없으니, 이미 근심하면 허물이 없을 것이다.
64는 지극하게 임하는 것이니, 허물이 없다.
65는 지혜롭게 임하는 것이니, 대군의 마땅함이니 길하다.
상6은 돈후하게 임하는 것이니, 길하여 허물이 없다.

Lin indicates that under the conditions supposed in it there will be great progress and success, while it will be advantageous to be firmly correct. In the eighth month there will be evil.

1. F9, undivided, shows its subject advancing in company with the subject of the second line. Through his firm correctness there will be good fortune.
2. 92, undivided, shows its subject advancing in company with the subject of the first line. There will be good fortune; advancing will be in every way advantageous.
3. 63, divided, shows one well pleased indeed to advance, but whose action will be in no way advantageous. If he become anxious about it however, there will be no error.
4. 64, divided, shows one advancing in the highest mode. There will be no error.
5. 65, divided, shows the advance of wisdom, such as befits the great ruler. There will be good fortune.
6. L6, divided, shows the advance of honesty and generosity. There will be evil. there will be calamities and errors. If with his views he put the hosts in motion, the end will be a great defeat, whose issues will extend to the ruler of the state. Even in ten years he will not be able to repair the disaster.

地風 觀 ⑳

觀、盥而不薦、有孚顒若。

象曰、大觀、在上、順而巽、中正、以觀天下。觀盥而不薦有孚顒若、下觀而化也。觀天之神道而四時不忒、聖人、以神道設教而天下、服矣。

象曰、風行地上、觀、先王、以、省方觀民、設教。

初六、童觀、小人、无咎、君子、吝。象曰、初六童觀、小人道也。

六二、闚觀、利女貞。象曰、闚觀女貞、亦可醜也。

六三、觀我生、進退。象曰、觀我生進退、未失道也。

六四、觀國之光、利用賓于王。象曰、觀國之光、尚賓也。

九五、觀我生、君子、无咎。象曰、觀我生、觀民也。

上九、觀其生、君子、无咎。象曰、觀其生、志未平也。

관觀은 손을 씻고서 아직 제물을 올리지 않으면 믿음이 있어서 엄숙할 것이다.

초6은 아이가 보는 것이니, 소인은 허물이 없고 군자는 궁색하다.
62는 문틈으로 엿보는 것이니, 여자의 곧음이 이롭다.
63은 나의 움직임을 보아서 나아가고 물러간다.
64는 나라의 광채를 봄이니, 왕에게 손님대접을 받는 것이 이롭다.
95는 나의 움직임을 보되 군자라면 허물이 없을 것이다.
상9는 그 움직임이 보되, 군자면 허물이 없을 것이다.

Guan shows how he whom it represents should be like the worshipper who has washed his hands, but not yet presented his offerings:- with sincerity and an appearance of dignity commanding reverent regard.

1. F6, divided, shows the looking of a lad;- not blamable in men of inferior rank, but matter for regret in superior men.
2. 62, divided, shows one peeping out from a door. It would be advantageous if it were merely the firm correctness of a female.
3. 63, divided, shows one looking at the course of his own life, to advance or recede accordingly.
4. 64, divided, shows one contemplating the glory of the kingdom. It will be advantageous for him, being such as he is, to seek to be a guest of the king.
5. 95, undivided, shows its subject contemplating his own life - course. A superior man, he will thus fall into no error.
6. L9, undivided, shows its subject contemplating his character to see if it be indeed that of a superior man. He will not fall into error.

雷火 ䷔ 嗑噬 (二一)

噬嗑、亨、利用獄。

彖曰、頤中有物、曰噬嗑。噬嗑而亨、剛柔分、動而明、雷電、合而章。柔得中而上行、雖不當位、利用獄也。

象曰、雷電、噬嗑、先王、以、明罰勑法。

初九、屨校、滅趾、无咎。象曰、屨校滅趾、不行也。

六二、噬膚、滅鼻、无咎。象曰、噬膚滅鼻、乘剛也。

六三、噬腊肉、遇毒、小吝、无咎。象曰、遇毒、位不當也。

九四、噬乾胏、得金矢、利艱貞、吉。象曰、利艱貞吉、未光也。

六五、噬乾肉、得黃金、貞厲、无咎。象曰、貞厲无咎、得當也。

上九、何校、滅耳、凶。象曰、何校滅耳、聰不明也。

서합噬嗑은 형통하니 형옥刑獄을 씀이 이로울 것이다.

초9는 형틀을 신겨 발을 못 쓰게 하지만, 허물은 없다.
62는 살을 깨물어 코를 상하게 하지만 허물은 없다.
63은 말린 고기를 씹다가 독을 만나니, 조금 궁색하지만 허물은 없다.
94는 뼈가 붙은 마른 고기를 씹다가 쇠화살을 얻으니, 어려워도 곧음이 이로우니 길할 것이다.
65는 마른 고기를 씹다가 황금을 얻으니, 곧게 하고 두려워하면 허물이 없을 것이다.
상9는 형틀에 매여서 귀를 다치니 흉하다.

Shike indicates successful progress in the condition of things which it supposes. It will be advantageous to use legal constraints.

1. F9, undivided, shows one with his feet in the stocks and deprived of his toes. There will be no error.
2. 62, divided, shows one biting through the soft flesh, and going on to bite off the nose. There will be no error.
3. 63, divided, shows one gnawing dried flesh, and meeting with what is disagreeable. There will be occasion for some small regret, but no great error.
4. 94, undivided, shows one gnawing the flesh dried on the bone, and getting the pledges of money and arrows. It will be advantageous to him to realise the difficulty of his task and be firm ,- in which case there will be good fortune.
5. 65, divided, shows one gnawing at dried flesh, and finding the yellow gold. Let him be firm and correct, realising the peril of his position. There will be no error.
6. L9, undivided, shows one wearing the cangue, and deprived of his ears. There will be evil.

火山 ䷕ 賁 ㉒

賁、亨、小利有攸往。

彖曰、賁亨、柔來而文剛故、亨、分剛、上而文柔故、小利有攸往。天文也、文明以止、人文也。觀乎天文、以察時變、觀乎人文、以化成天下。

象曰、山下有火、賁、君子以、明庶政、无敢折獄。

初九、賁其趾、舍車而徒。象曰、舍車而徒、義弗乘也。

六二、賁其須。象曰、賁其須、與上興也。

九三、賁如濡如、永貞、吉。象曰、永貞之吉、終莫之陵也。

六四、賁如皤如、白馬翰如、匪寇、婚媾。象曰、六四、當位疑也、匪寇婚媾、終无尤也。

六五、賁于丘園、束帛戔戔、吝、終吉。象曰、六五之吉、有喜也。

上九、白賁、无咎。象曰、白賁无咎、上得志也。

비賁는 형통하니, 갈 바가 있으면 조금 이로울 것이다.

초9는 그 발꿈치를 꾸미니, 수레를 버리고 걸어간다.
62는 그 수염을 장식하는 것이다.
93은 꾸미고 윤택하니, 오래도록 바르게 하면 길할 것이다.
64는 꾸민 듯 꾸미지 않은 듯하며, 흰말이 머뭇거리니, 도적이 아니라 혼인을 청하는 것이다.
65는 동산을 꾸미는 것이니, 비단 묶음이 작으면 궁색하나 마침내 길할 것이다.
상9는 희게 꾸미면 허물이 없을 것이다.

Bi indicates that there should be free course in what it denotes. There will be little advantage however if it be allowed to advance and take the lead.

1. F9, undivided, shows one adorning the way of his feet. He can discard a carriage and walk on foot.
2. 62, divided, shows one adorning his beard.
3. 93, undivided, shows its subject with the appearance of being adorned and bedewed with rich favours. But let him ever maintain his firm correctness, and there will be good fortune.
4. 64, divided, shows one looking as if adorned, but only in white. As if mounted on a white horse, and furnished with wings, he seeks union with the subject of the first line, while the intervening third pursues, not as a robber, but intent on a matrimonial alliance.
5. 65, divided, shows its subject adorned by the occupants of the heights and gardens. He bears his roll of silk, small and slight. He may appear stingy; but there will be good fortune in the end.
6. L9, undivided, shows one with white as his onlyornament. There will be no error.

地山 ䷖ 剝 (二三)

剝、不利有攸往。

象曰、剝、剝也、柔變剛也。不利有攸往、小人、長也。順而止之、觀象也、君子尚消息盈虛、天行也。

象曰、山附於地、剝、上、以、厚下、安宅。

初六、剝牀以足、蔑貞、凶。象曰、剝牀以足、以滅下也。

六二、剝牀以辨、蔑貞、凶。象曰、剝牀以辨、未有與也。

六三、剝之无咎。象曰、剝之无咎、失上下也。

六四、剝牀以膚、凶。象曰、剝牀以膚、切近災也。

六五、貫魚、以宮人寵、无不利。象曰、以宮人寵、終无尤也。

上九、碩果不食、君子、得輿、小人、剝廬。象曰、君子得輿、民所載也、小人剝廬、終不可用也。

박剝은 가는 바를 둠이 이롭지 않다.

초6은 평상의 다리를 깎으니, 바른 것을 없애는 것이라 흉하다.
62는 평상의 언저리를 깎으니, 바른 것을 없애는 것이라 흉하다.
63은 깎지만 허물이 없다.
64는 평상을 깎아서 피부에 닿으니 흉하다.
65는 고기를 꿰어서 궁인宮人을 총애하듯이 하면 이롭지 않음이 없다.
상9는 큰 과일을 먹지 않으니, 군자는 수레를 얻고, 소인은 집을 빼앗길 것이다.

Bao indicates that in the state which it symbolises it will not be advantageous to make a movement in any direction whatever.

1. F6, divided, shows one overturning the couch by injuring its legs. The injury will go on to the destruction of all firm correctness, and there will be evil.
2. 62, divided, shows one overthrowing the couch by injuring its frame. The injury will go on to the destruction of all firm correctness, and there will be evil.
3. 63, divided, shows its subject among the overthrowers; but there will be no error.
4. 64, divided, shows its subject having overthrown the couch, and going to injure the skin of him who lies on it. There will be evil.
5. 65, divided, shows its subject leading on the others like a string of fishes, and obtaining for them the favour that lights on the inmates of the palace. There will be advantage in every way.
6. L9, undivided, shows its subject as a great fruit which has not been eaten. The superior man finds the people again as a chariot carrying him. The small men by their course overthrow their own dwellings.

雷地 ䷗ 復 ㉔

復、亨。出入、无疾、朋來、无咎、反復其道、七日、來復。利有攸往。

象曰、復亨、剛反、動而以順行、是以出入无疾朋來无咎。反復其道七日來復、天行也。利有攸往、剛長也。復、其見天地之心乎？

象曰、雷在地中、復、先王、以、至日、閉關、商旅不行、后不省方。

初九、不遠復、无祗悔、元吉。象曰、不遠之復、以脩身也。

六二、休復、吉。象曰、休復之吉、以下仁也。

六三、頻復、厲、无咎。象曰、頻復之厲、義无咎也。

六四、中行、獨復。象曰、中行獨復、以從道也。

六五、敦復、无悔。象曰、敦復无悔、中以自考也。

上六、迷復、凶、有災眚。用行師、終有大敗、以其國、君、凶、至于十年、不克征。象曰、迷復之凶、反君道也。

복復은 형통하여 출입에 병통이 없으니, 벗이 와야 허물이 없을 것이다. 그 도를 반복해서 칠일만에 회복하니, 갈 바를 둠이 이롭다.

초9는 머지않아 돌아오는 것이다. 후회하는데 이르지 않으니, 크게 길할 것이다.
62는 아름답게 돌아오니 길하다.
63은 찡그리며 돌아오니, 위태하지만 허물은 없을 것이다.
64는 가운데서 행하지만, 홀로 돌아올 것이다.
65는 돈독하게 돌아오니, 후회가 없을 것이다.
상6은 혼미하게 돌아오니 흉하다. 재앙이 있어 군사를 쓰면 마침내 크게 패하고, 그 나라를 걸면 임금이 흉하여 십년이 되도록 이기지 못할 것이다.

Fu indicates that there will be free course and progress in what it denotes. The subject of it finds no one to distress him in his exits and entrances; friends come to him, and no error is committed. He will return and repeat his proper course. In seven days comes his return. There will be advantage in whatever direction movement is made.

1. F9, undivided, shows its subject returning from an error of no great extent, which would not proceed to anything requiring repentance. There will be great good fortune.
2. 62, divided, shows the admirable return of its subject. There will be good fortune.
3. 63, divided, shows one who has made repeated returns. The position is perilous, but there will be no error.
4. 64, divided, shows its subject moving right in the centre among those represented by the other divided lines, and yet returning alone to his proper path.
5. 65, divided, shows the noble return of its subject. There will be no ground for repentance.
6. L6, divided, shows its subject all astray on the subject of returning. There will be evil. There will be calamities and errors. If with his views he put the hosts in motion, the end will be a great defeat, whose issues will extend to the ruler of the state. Even in ten years he will not be able to repair the disaster.

天雷 无妄 (二五)

无妄、元亨、利貞、其匪正、有眚、不利有攸往。

彖曰、无妄、剛、自外來而爲主於內、動而健、剛中而應、大亨以正、天之命也。其匪正有眚不利有攸往、无妄之往、何之矣？天命不祐、行矣哉！

象曰、天下雷行、物與无妄、先王、以、茂對時、育萬物。

初九、无妄、往、吉。象曰、无妄之往、得志也。

六二、不耕、穫、不菑、畬、則利有攸往。象曰、不耕穫、未富也。

六三、无妄之災、或繫之牛、行人之得、邑人之災。象曰、行人得牛、邑人災也。

九四、可貞、无咎。象曰、可貞无咎、固有之也。

九五、无妄之疾、勿藥、有喜。象曰、无妄之藥、不可試也。

上九、无妄、行、有眚、无攸利。象曰、无妄之行、窮之災也。

무망无妄은 크게 형통하고 곧음이 이로우니, 그것이 바르지 않으면 재앙이 있을 것이다. 갈 곳은 있으나 이롭지 않을 것이다.

초9는 망령됨이 없으니, 가는 것이 길할 것이다.
62는 경작하지 않고도 수확하며, 개간하지 않고도 좋은 밭을 만드니, 갈 곳이 있으면 이로울 것이다.
63은 무망无妄의 재앙이니, 소를 묶어두었으나, 관리를 공을 얻고 읍인邑人은 재앙을 얻는다.
94는 바르게 할 수 있으니, 허물이 없을 것이다.
95는 무망无妄의 병은 약을 쓰지 않으면 기쁨이 있을 것이다.
상9는 망령됨이 없는데도 간다면 재앙이 있어서 이로울 것이 없을 것이다.

Wuwang indicates great progress and success, while there will be advantage in being firm and correct. If its subject and his action be not correct, he will fall into errors, and it will not be advantageous for him to move in any direction.

1. F9, undivided, shows its subject free from all insincerity. His advance will be accompanied with good fortune.
2. 62, divided, shows one who reaps without having ploughed that he might reap, and gathers the produce of his third year's fields without having cultivated them the first year for that end. To such a one there will be advantage in whatever direction he may move,
3. 63, divided, shows calamity happening to one who is free from insincerity ;- as in the case of an ox that has been tied up. A passer by finds it and carries it off, while the people in the neighbourhood have the calamity of being accused and apprehended.
4. 94, undivided, shows a case in which, if its subject can remain firm and correct, there will be no error.
5. 95, undivided, shows one who is free from insincerity, and yet has fallen ill. Let him not use medicine, and he will have occasion for joy in his recovery.
6. L9, undivided, shows its subject free from insincerity, yet sure to fall into error, if he take action. His action will not be advantageous in any way.

天山 ☶☰ 大畜 (二六)

大畜、利貞、不家食、吉、利涉大川。

象曰、大畜、剛健、篤實、輝光、日新其德、剛上而尚賢、能止健、大正也。不家食吉、養賢也。利涉大川、應乎天也。

象曰、天在山中、大畜、君子以、多識前言往行、以畜其德。

初九、有厲、利已。象曰、有厲利已、不犯災也。

九二、輿說輹。象曰、輿說輹、中、无尤也。

九三、良馬逐、利艱貞、曰閑輿衛、利有攸往。象曰、利有攸往、上、合志也。

六四、童牛之牿、元吉。象曰、六四元吉、有喜也。

六五、豶豕之牙、吉。象曰、六五之吉、有慶也。

上九、何天之衢、亨。象曰、何天之衢、道大行也。

대축大畜은 바르게 함이 이로우니, 집에서 먹지 아니 하면 길하고, 큰 내를 건넘이 이로울 것이다.

초9는 위태로움이 있으니, 그침이 이롭다.
92는 수레의 바퀴가 벗겨진다.
93은 좋은 말로 쫓는 것이니 어려워도 바르게 함이 이롭다. 수레가 막힌 데를 만났으나 호위하니 가는 바 있음이 이롭다.
64는 송아지의 빗장이니, 크게 길할 것이다.
65는 돼지의 어금니를 거세하니, 길할 것이다.
상9는 어찌 그치리오? 하늘의 길이 트일 것이다.

Under the conditions of *Daxu* it will be advantageous to be firm and correct. If its subject do not seek to enjoy his revenues in his own family without taking service at court, there will be good fortune. It will be advantageous for him to cross the great stream.

1. F9, undivided, shows its subject in a position of peril. It will be advantageous for him to stop his advance.
2. 92, undivided, shows a carriage with the strap under it removed.
3. 93, undivided shows its subject urging his way with good horses. It will be advantageous for him to realise the difficulty of his course, and to be firm and correct, exercising himself daily in his charioteering and methods of defence; then there will be advantage in whatever direction he may advance.
4. 64, divided, shows the young bull, and yet having the piece of wood over his horns. There will be great good fortune.
5. 65, divided, shows the teeth of a castrated hog. There will be good fortune.
6. L9, undivided, shows its subject as in command of the firmament of heaven. There will be progress.

雷山 ䷚ 頤 (二七)

頤、貞、吉、觀頤、自求口實。

象曰、頤貞吉、養正則吉也。觀頤、觀其所養也、自求口實、觀其自養也。天地養萬物、聖人、養賢、以及萬民、頤之時大矣哉！

象曰、山下有雷、頤、君子以、愼言語、節飮食。

初九、舍爾靈龜、觀我朶頤、凶。象曰、觀我朶頤、亦不足貴也。

六二、顚頤、拂經、于丘、頤、征、凶。象曰、六二征凶、行、失類也。

六三、拂頤貞、凶、十年勿用、无攸利。象曰、十年勿用、道大悖也。

六四、顚頤、吉、虎視耽耽、其欲逐逐、无咎。象曰、顚頤之吉、上施光也。

六五、拂經、居貞、吉、不可涉大川。象曰、居貞之吉、順以從上也。

上九、由頤、厲、吉、利涉大川。象曰、由頤厲吉、大有慶也。

이頤는 바르면 길하니 턱을 보며 스스로 먹을 것을 구한다.

초9는 너의 신령한 거북을 버리고 내가 음식을 씹는 것을 바라보니 흉하다.
62는 거꾸로 기르는 것이다. 항상 의義를 거스리니, 기르면서 가면 흉할 것이다.
63은 기름의 바름을 거스려 흉하니 십년이라도 쓰이지 못니 이로울 것이 없다.
64는 거꾸로 기르나 길하니, 호랑이가 먹이를 노려보는 듯 하다. 그 의욕이 끊기지 않으면 허물이 없을 것이다.
65는 의義를 거스리나 바르게 지키고 있으면 길하다. 큰 내를 건널 수 없을 것이다.
상9는 말미암아 길러주니, 엄정히 하면 길하다. 큰 내를 건너는 것이 이롭다.

Yi indicates that with firm correctness there will be good fortune in what is denoted by it. We must look at what we are seeking to nourish, and by the exercise of our thoughts seek for the proper aliment.

1. F9, undivided, seems to be thus addressed, 'you leave your efficacious tortoise, and look at me till your lower jaw hangs down.' there will be evil.
2. 62, Divided, shows one looking downwards for nourishment, which is contrary to what is proper; or seeking it form the hight above, advance towards which will lead to evil.
3. 63, divided, shows one acting contrary to the method of nourishing. However firm he may be, there will be evil. For ten years let him not take any action, for it will not be in any way advantageous.
4. 64, divided, shows one looking downwards for the power to nourish. There will be good fortune. Looking with a tiger's downward unwavering glare, and with his desire that impels him to spring after spring, he will fall into no error.
5. 65, divided, shows one acting contrary to what is regular and proper; but if he abide in firmness, there will be good fortune. He should not, however, try to cross the great stream.
6. L9, undivided, shows him form whom comes the nourishing. His position is perilous, but there will be good fortune. It will be advantageous to cross the great stream.

風澤 ䷛ 大過 ㉘

大過、棟、撓、利有攸往、亨。

彖曰、大過、大者過也、棟撓、本末、弱也。剛過而中。巽而說行、利有攸往、乃亨。大過之時、大矣哉!

象曰、澤滅木、大過、君子以、獨立不懼、遯世无悶。

初六、藉用白茅、无咎。象曰、藉用白茅、柔在下也。

九二、枯楊、生稊、老夫得其女妻、无不利。象曰、老夫女妻、過以相與也。

九三、棟、橈、凶。象曰、棟橈之凶、不可以有輔也。

九四、棟隆、吉、有它、吝。象曰、棟隆之吉、不橈乎下也。

九五、枯楊、生華、老婦得其士夫、无咎、无譽。象曰、枯楊生華、何可久也? 老婦士夫、亦可醜也。

上六、過涉滅頂、凶、无咎。象曰、過涉之凶、不可咎也。

대과大過는 기둥이 흔들리니 갈 바가 있어 이로우니 형통할 것이다.

초6은 자리를 까는데 흰 띠를 쓰니 허물이 없다.
92는 마른 버들에 싹이 나고 늙은이가 젊은 아내를 얻으니, 이롭지 않음이 없다.
93은 기둥이 흔들리니 흉하다.
94는 기둥이 높아서 길하지만, 다른 궁색함이 있을 것이다.
95는 마른 버드나무가 꽃을 피우고 늙은 지어미가 젊은 장부를 얻으니, 허물은 없지만 명예도 없을 것이다.
상6은 무리하게 하천을 건너다 이마까지 빠졌으니 흉하지만 허물은 없을 것이다.

Daguo suggests to us a beam that is weak. There will be advantage in moving under its conditions in any direction whatever; there will be success.

1. F6, divided, shows one placing mats of the white mâo grass under things set on the ground. There will be no error.
2. 92, undivided, shows a decayed willow producing shoots, or an old husband in possession of his young wife. There will be advantage in every way.
3. 93, undivided, shows a beam that is weak. There will be evil.
4. 94, undivided, shows a beam curving upwards. There will be good fortune. If the subject of it looks for other help but that of line one, there will be cause for regret.
5. 95, undivided, shows a decayed willow producing flowers, or an old wife in possession of her young husband. There will be occasion neither for blame nor for praise.
6. L6, divided, shows its subject with extraordinary boldness wading through a stream, till the water hides the crown of his head. There will be evil, but no ground for blame.

二九 習坎 ䷜ 重水

習坎、有孚、維心亨、行、有尚。

象曰、習坎、重險也、水流而不盈。行險而不失其信、維心亨、乃以剛中也、行有尚、往有功也。天險、不可升也、地險、山川丘陵也、王公設險、以守其國、險之時用、大矣哉！

象曰、水洊至習坎、君子以、常德行、習教事。

初六、習坎、入于坎窞、凶。象曰、習坎入坎、失道、凶也。

九二、坎、有險、求、小得。象曰、求小得、未出中也。

六三、來之、坎坎、險、且枕、入于坎窞、勿用。象曰、來之坎坎、終无功也。

六四、樽酒、簋貳、用缶、納約自牖、終无咎。象曰、樽酒簋貳、剛柔際也。

九五、坎不盈、祇既平、无咎。象曰、坎不盈、中、未大也。

上六、係用徽纆、寘于叢棘、三歲、不得、凶。象曰、上六失道、凶三歲也。

감坎을 익히면 믿음이 있어서 마음이 형통하리니, 행하면 숭상함이 있을 것이다.

초6은 험난한 일을 익혀 구덩이에 빠졌으니 흉하다.
92는 구덩이에 험난함이 있으나 구함을 조금 얻을 것이다.
63은 오고 감에 모두 구덩이뿐이다. 험한 데에 걸려서 깊은 구덩이 속으로 빠지니 움직이지 말라.
64는 한잔의 술과 음식을 질그릇으로 담아서 들창으로 간략하게 드리면, 마침내 허물이 없을 것이다.
95는 구덩이가 차지 아니하니, 평평한 데 이르면 허물이 없을 것이다.
상6은 끊으로 묶어 가시덩굴에 두어서 삼년 동안 얻을 수 없으니 흉하다.

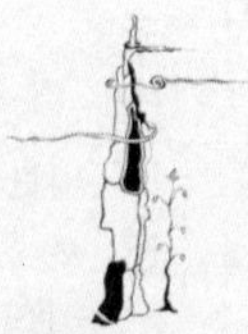

Kan, here repeated, shows the possession of sincerity, through which the mind is penetrating. Action in accordance with this will be of high value.

1. F6, divided, shows its subject in the double defile, and yet entering a cavern within it. There will be evil.
2. 92, undivided, shows its subject in all The peril of the defile. He will, however, get a little of the deliverance that he seeks.
3. 63, divided, shows its subject, whether he comes or goes =descends or ascends, confronted by a defile. All is peril to him and unrest. His endeavours will lead him into the cavern of the pit. There should be no action in such a case.
4. 64, divided, shows its subject at a feast, with simply a bottle of spirits, and a subsidiary basket of rice, while the cups and bowls are only of earthenware. He introduces his important lessons as his ruler's intelligence admits. There will in the end be no error.
5. 95, undivided, shows the water of the defile not yet full, so that it might flow away; but order will soon be brought about. There will be no error.
6. L6, divided, shows its subject bound with cords of three strands or two strands, and placed in the thicket of thorns. But in three years he does not learn the course for him to pursue. There will be evil.

火重 ䷝ 離 (三十)

離、利貞、亨、畜牝牛、吉。

彖曰、離、麗也。日月麗乎天、百穀草木、麗乎土。重明以麗乎正、乃化成天下、柔麗乎中正故、亨、是以畜牝牛吉也。

象曰、明兩、作離、大人以繼明、照于四方。

初九、履錯然、敬之、无咎。象曰、履錯之敬、以辟咎也。

六二、黃離、元吉。象曰、黃離元吉、得中道也。

九三、日昃之離、不鼓缶而歌、則大耋之嗟、凶。象曰、日昃之離、何可久也！

九四、突如其來如、焚如、死如、棄如。象曰、突如其來如、无所容也。

六五、出涕沱若、戚嗟若、吉。象曰、六五之吉、離王公也。

上九、王用出征、有嘉、折首、獲匪其醜、无咎。象曰、王用出征、以正邦也。

이離는 곧음이 이롭고 형통하니, 암소를 기르면 길할 것이다.

초9는 밟는 것이 조심스러우니, 공경하면 허물이 없을 것이다.
62는 누렇게 걸리니 크게 길할 것이다.
93은 해가 기울어져 걸림이니, 질그릇을 두드리고 노래하지 않으면, 늙은이가 탄식하니 흉할 것이다.
94는 돌연히 오는 듯하다. 불사르는 듯하니, 죽은 듯하고 버린 듯하다.
65는 눈물이 비오는 듯하며 슬퍼서 탄식하니, 길할 것이다.
상9는 왕이 직접 출정하면 좋은 결과가 있을 것이니, 우두머리를 베고 동류가 아닌 자들을 잡으면 허물이 없을 것이다.

Li indicates that, in regard to what it denotes, it will be advantageous to be firm and correct, and that thus there will be free course and success. Let its subject also nourish a docility like that of the cow, and there will be good fortune.

1. F9, undivided, shows one ready to move with confused steps. But he treads at the same time reverently, and there will be no mistake.
2. 62, divided, shows its subject in his place in yellow. There will be great good fortune.
3. 93, undivided, shows its subject in a position like that of the declining sun. Instead of playing on his instrument of earthenware, and singing to it, he utters the groans of an old man of eighty. There will be evil.
4. 94, undivided, shows the manner of its subject's coming. How abrupt it is, as with fire, with death, to be rejected by all!
5. 65, divided, shows its subject as one with tears flowing in torrents, and groaning in sorrow. There will be good fortune.
6. L9, undivided, shows the king employing its subject in his punitive expeditions. Achieving admirable merit, he breaks only the chiefs of the rebels. Where his prisoners were not their associates, he does not punish. There will be no error.

주역

下經

山澤 ䷞ 咸 ㉜

咸、亨、利貞、取女、吉。

象曰、咸、感也、柔上而剛下、二氣感應以相與。止而說、男下女、是以亨、利貞、取女吉也。天地感而萬物化生、聖人感人心而天下和平、觀其所感、而天地萬物之情、可見矣！

象曰、山上有澤、咸、君子以虛受人。

初六、咸其拇。象曰、咸其拇、志在外也。

六二、咸其腓、凶、居、吉。象曰、雖凶居吉、順不害也。

九三、咸其股、執其隨、往吝。象曰、咸其股、亦不處也、志在隨人、所執、下也。

九四、貞吉、悔亡、憧憧往來、朋從爾思。象曰、貞吉悔亡、未感害也、憧憧往來、未光大也。

九五、咸其脢、无悔。象曰、咸其脢、志末也。

上六、咸其輔頰舌。象曰、咸其輔頰舌、滕口說也。

함咸은 형통하니 곧음이 이로우며, 여자를 취하면 길할 것이다.

초6은 그 엄지발가락을 느끼는 것이다.
62는 그 장딴지를 느끼면 흉하고, 가만히 있으면 길하다.
93은 그 다리를 느끼는 것이니, 사람을 좇아다니는 뜻을 가진다. 가면 궁색할 것이다.
94는 곧으면 길하여 후회가 없을 것이니, 이리저리 왕래하고서야 벗이 네 생각을 따를 것이다.
95는 그 등을 느끼는 것이니, 후회가 없을 것이다.
상6은 그 볼과 뺨과 혀로 느끼는 것이다.

Xian indicates that, on the fulfilment of the conditions in it, there will be free course and success. Its advantageousness will depend on the being firm and correct, as in marrying a young lady. There will be good fortune.

1. F6, divided, shows one moving his great toes.
2. 62, divided, shows one moving the calves of his leg. There will be evil. If he abide quiet in his place, there will be good fortune.
3. 93, undivided, shows one moving his thighs, and keeping close hold of those whom he follows. Going forward in this way will cause regret.
4. 94, undivided, shows that firm correctness which will lead to good fortune, and prevent all occasion for repentance. If its subject be unsettled in his movements, only his friends will follow his purpose.
5. 95, undivided, shows one moving the flesh along the spine above the heart. There will be no occasion for repentance.
6. L6, divided, shows one moving his jaws and tongue.

風雷 ䷟ 恒 (三二)

恒、亨、无咎、利貞、利有攸往。

彖曰、恒、久也。剛上而柔下、雷風、相與、巽而動、剛柔皆應、恒。恒亨无咎利貞、久於其道也。天地之道、恒久而不已也。利有攸往、終則有始也。日月得天而能久照、四時變化而能久成、聖人久於其道而天下化成、觀其所恒、而天地萬物之情、可見矣！

象曰、雷風、恒、君子以立不易方。

初六、浚恒、貞、凶、无攸利。象曰、浚恒之凶、始求深也。

九二、悔亡。象曰、九二悔亡、能久中也。

九三、不恒其德、或承之羞、貞、吝。象曰、不恒其德、无所容也。

九四、田无禽。象曰、久非其位、安得禽也

六五、恒其德、貞、婦人吉、夫子凶。象曰、婦人貞吉、從一而終也、夫子制義、從婦凶也。

上六、振恒、凶。象曰、振恒在上、大无功也。

항상 형통하고 허물이 없어야 이롭고 곧으며, 갈 곳이 있으면 이로울 것이다.

초6은 항상 파고들려 하므로, 곧게 하여도 흉하여 이로움이 없다.
92는 후회가 없을 것이다.
93은 그 덕을 항상 지키지 못하는 것이니, 혹 부끄러움을 받아서 곧게 하더라도 궁색할 것이다.
94는 사냥하려는데 새가 없다.
65는 그 덕을 항상 지키면 곧으니, 부인은 길하고 남자는 흉하다.
상6은 항구한 것을 흔드니 흉하다.

Heng indicates successful progress and no error in what it denotes. But the advantage will come from being firm and correct; and movement in any direction whatever will be advantageous.

1. F6, divided, shows its subject deeply desirous of long continuance. Even with firm correctness there will be evil; there will be no advantage in any way.
2. 92, undivided, shows all occasion for repentance disappearing.
3. 93, undivided, shows one who does not continuously maintain his virtue. There are those who will impute this to him as a disgrace.
   However firm he may be, there will be ground for regret.
4. 94, undivided, shows a field where there is no game.
5. 65, divided, shows its subject continuously maintaining the virtue indicated by it. In a wife this will be frtunate; in a husband, evil.
6. L6, divided, shows its sibject exciting himself to long continuance. There will be evil.

山天 ䷠ 遯 (三三)

遯、亨、小利貞。

象曰、遯亨、遯而亨也、剛當位而應、與時行也。小利貞、浸而長也。遯之時義大矣哉。

象曰、天下有山、遯、君子以遠小人、不惡而嚴。

初六、遯尾、厲、勿用有攸往。象曰、遯尾之厲、不往、何災也?

六二、執之用黃牛之革、莫之勝說。象曰、執用黃牛、固志也。

九三、係遯、有疾厲、畜臣妾、吉。象曰、係遯之厲、有疾憊也、畜臣妾吉、不可大事也。

九四、好遯、君子吉、小人否。象曰、君子好遯、小人否也。

九五、嘉遯、貞、吉。象曰、嘉遯貞吉、以正志也。

上九、肥遯、无不利。象曰、肥遯无不利、无所疑也。

돈遯은 형통하니 곧게 하는 것이 조금 이롭다.

초6은 물러가는 꼬리라 위태로우니, 가지말 것이다
62는 황소의 가죽을 써서 잡아맨 것이니, 벗길 수 없다.
93은 물러나려고 하나 매어져 있다. 병이 있어 위태로우니, 신하와 첩을 기르는 것이 길할 것이다.
94는 좋아도 물러나는 것이니, 군자는 길하지만 소인은 그렇지 않을 것이다.
95는 아름답게 물러나는 것이니, 바르게 하면 길할 것이다.
상9는 여유 있게 물러가는 것이니, 이롭지 않음이 없다.

Dun indicates successful progress in its circumstances. To a small extent it will still be advantageous to be firm and correct.

1. F6, divided, shows a retiring tail. The position is perilous. No movement in any direction should be made.
2. 62, divided, shows its subject holding his purpose fast as if by a thong made from the hide of a yellow ox, which cannot be broken.
3. 93, undivided, shows one retiring but bound, -to his distress and peril. If he were to deal with his binders as in nourishing a servant or concubine, it would be fortunate for him.
4. 94, undivided, shows its subject retiring notwithstanding his likings. In a superior man this will lead to good fortune; a small man cannot attain to this.
5. 95, undivided, shows its subject retiring in an admirable way. With firm correctness there will be good fortune.
6. L9, undivided, shows its subject retiring in a noble way. It will be advantageous in every respect.

天雷 ䷡ 大壯 (三四)

大壯、利貞。

象曰、大壯、大者壯也、剛以動、故壯。大壯利貞、大者正也。正大而天地之情、可見矣！

象曰、雷在天上、大壯、君子以非禮弗履。

初九、壯于趾、征、凶、有孚。象曰、壯於趾、其孚窮也。

九二、貞吉。象曰、九二貞吉、以中也。

九三、小人用壯、君子用罔、貞、厲、羝羊觸藩、羸其角。象曰、小人用壯、君子罔也。

九四、貞、吉、悔亡、藩決不羸、壯于大輿之輹。象曰、藩決不羸、尚往也。

六五、喪羊于易、无悔。象曰、喪羊于易、位不當也。

上六、羝羊觸藩、不能退、不能遂、无攸利、艱則吉。象曰、不能退、不能遂、不詳也、艱則吉、咎不長也。

대장大壯은 곧게 함이 이로울 것이다.

초9는 발꿈치가 씩씩하니, 가면 흉할 것이 틀림없다.
92는 곧게 하여 길할 것이다.
93은 소인이 장함을 쓰고 군자는 그물을 쓰니, 곧게 하더라도 위태하다. 숫양이 울타리를 들이받아 그 뿔이 걸린다.
94는 바르게 하면 길하여 후회가 없을 것이니, 울타리가 터져서 걸리지 아니하며, 큰 수레의 바퀴가 씩씩하게 굴러갈 것이다.
65는 양羊을 쉽게 잃으면 후회가 없을 것이다.
상6은 숫양이 울타리에 걸려 물러나지도 나아가지도 못해 이로운 바가 없으니, 어려움을 견디면 길할 것이다.

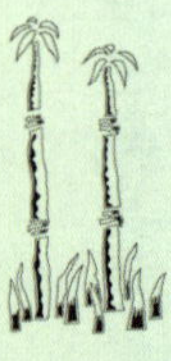

Dazhuang indicates that under the conditions which it symbolises it will be advantageous to be firm and correct.

1. F9, undivided, shows its subject manifesting his strength in his toes. But advance will lead to evil,- most certainly.
2. 92, undivided, shows that with firm correctness there will be good fortune.
3. 93, undivided, shows, in the case of a small man, one using all his strength; and in the case of a superior man firm correctness the position would be perilous. The exercise of strength in it might be compared to the case of a ram butting against a fence, and getting his horns entangled.
4. 94, undivided, shows a case in which firm correctness leads to good fortune, and occasion for repentance disappears. We see the fence opened without the horns being entangled. The strength is like that in the wheel-spokes of a large waggon.
5. 65, divided, shows one who loses his ram-like strength in the ease of his position. But there will be no occasion for repentance.
6. L6, divided, shows one who may be compared to the ram butting against the fence, and unable either to retreat, or to advance as he would fain do. There will not be advantage in any respect; but if he realise the difficulty of his position, there will be good fortune.

地火 ䷢ 晋 ㊂㊄

晋、康侯、用錫馬蕃庶、晝日三接。

象曰、晋、進也、明出地上。順而麗乎大明、柔進而上行、是以康侯用錫馬蕃庶、晝日三接也。

象曰、明出地上、晋、君子以自昭明德。

初六、晋如摧如、貞吉、罔孚、裕、无咎。象曰、晋如摧如、獨行正也、裕无咎、未受命。

六二、晋如愁如、貞吉、受茲介福于其王母。象曰、受茲介福、以中正也。

六三、衆允、悔亡。象曰、衆允之志、上行也。

九四、晋如鼫鼠、貞厲。象曰、鼫鼠貞厲、位不當也。

六五、悔亡、失得勿恤、往吉、无不利。象曰、失得勿恤、往有慶也。

上九、晋其角、維用伐邑、厲吉、无咎、貞吝。象曰、維用伐邑、道未光也。

진晉은 훌륭한 제후에게 많은 말을 주고 낮에 세 번이나 접견하는 것이다.

초6은 나아가고 물러섬에 바르게 하면 길하고 믿음이 없더라도 여유로우면 허물이 없을 것이다.
62는 나아가는 것이 근심스럽지만 바르게 하면 길할 것이니, 큰 복을 왕모王母에게서 받을 것이다.
63은 무리가 믿으니, 후회가 없을 것이다.
94는 나아가는 것이 다람쥐와 같으니, 바르게 해도 위태로울 것이다.
65는 후회가 없으니, 잃고 얻음을 근심하지 말 것이다. 그대로 행하면 길하여 이롭지 않음이 없을 것이다.
상9는 그 뿔(끝)까지 나아가니, 이것으로 읍을 징벌하면 위태로우나, 길하고 허물이 없을 것이이다. 고집하면 궁색할 것이다.

In *Jin* we see a prince who secures the tranquillity of the people presented on that account with numerous horses by the king, and three times in a day received at interviews.

1. F6, divided, shows one wishing to advance, and at the same time kept back. Let him be firm and correct, and there will be good fortune. If trust be not reposed in him, let him maintain a large and generous mind, and there will be no error.
2. 62, divided, shows its subject with the appearance of advancing, and yet of being sorrowful. If he be firm and correct, there will be good fortune. He will receive this great blessing from his grandmother.
3. 63, divided, shows its subject trusted by all around him. All occasion for repentance will disappear.
4. 94, undivided, shows its subject with the appearance of advancing, but like a marmot. However firm and correct he may be, the position is one of peril.
5. 65, divided, shows how all occasion for repentance disappears from its subject. But let him not concern himself about whether he shall fail or succeed. To advance will be fortunate, and in every way advantageous.
6. L9, undivided, shows one advancing his horns. But he only uses them to punish the rebellious people of his own city. The position is perilous, but there will be good fortune. Yet however firm and correct he may be, there will be occasion for regret.

火地 ䷣ 明夷 (三六)

明夷、利艱貞。

彖曰、明入地中、明夷、內文明而外柔順、以蒙大難、文王以之。利艱貞、晦其明也、內難而能正其志、箕子以之。

象曰、明入地中、明夷、君子以蒞衆、用晦而明。

初九、明夷于飛、垂其翼、君子于行、三日不食。有攸往、主人有言。象曰、君子于行、義不食也。

六二、明夷、夷于左股、用拯馬壯、吉。象曰、六二之吉、順以則也。

九三、明夷于南狩、得其大首、不可疾貞。象曰、南狩之志、乃大得也。

六四、入于左腹、獲明夷之心、于出門庭。象曰、入于左腹、獲心意也。

六五、箕子之明夷、利貞。象曰、箕子之貞、明不可息也。

上六、不明晦、初登于天、後入于地。象曰、初登于天、照四國也、後入于地、失則也。

명이明夷는 어려워도 바르게 하면 이로울 것이다.

초9는 어두운 때에 날다가 그 날개를 늘어뜨리니, 것이니, 군자가 감에 사흘을 먹지 못 한다 감에 있어 주인이 할 말이 있다.

62는 어두운 때에 왼쪽 다리를 상하는 것이니, 구원하는 말이 건장하면 길할 것이다.

93은 어두운 때에 남쪽으로 사냥하여 그 우두머리를 얻으니, 빨리 바르게 할 수는 없을 것이다.

64는 왼쪽 배에 들어가서 명이의 마음을 얻어 문정門庭에서 나온다.

65는 기자箕子의 명이明夷니, 바르게 함이 이롭다.

상6은 밝지 않아서 어두우니, 처음에는 하늘에 오르고 뒤에는 땅에 들어간다.

Mingyi indicates that in the circumstances which it denotes it will be advantageous to realise the difficulty of the position, and maintain firm correctness.

1. F9, undivided, shows its subject, in the condition indicated by ming i, flying, but with drooping wings. When the superior man is revolving his going away, he may be for three days without eating. Wherever he goes, the people there may speak derisively of him.
2. 62, divided, shows its subject, in the condition indicated by ming i, wounded in the left thigh. He saves himself by the strength of a swift horse; and is fortunate.
3. 93, undivided, shows its subject, in the condition indicated by Ming I, hunting in the south, and taking the great chief of the darkness. He should not be eager to make all correct at once.
4. 64, divided, shows its subject just entered into the left side of the belly of the dark land. But he is able to carry out the mind appropriate in the condition indicated by Ming I, quitting the gate and courtyard of the lord of darkness.
5. 65, divided, shows how the count of ki fulfilled the condition indicated by Ming I. It will be advantageous to be firm and correct.
6. L6, divided, shows the case where there is no light, but only obscurity. Its subject had at first ascended to the top of the sky; his future shall be to go into the earth.

火風 ䷤ 人家 三七

家人、利女貞。

象曰、家人、女正位乎內、男正位乎外、男女正、天地之大義也。家人有嚴君焉、父母之謂也。父父、子子、兄兄、弟弟、夫夫、婦婦、而家道正、正家而天下定矣。

象曰、風自火出、家人、君子以言有物而行有恒。

初九、閑有家、悔亡。象曰、閑有家、志未變也。

六二、无攸遂、在中饋、貞吉。象曰、六二之吉、順以巽也。

九三、家人嗃嗃、悔厲、吉、婦子嘻嘻、終吝。象曰、家人嗃嗃、未失也、婦子嘻嘻、失家節也。

六四、富家、大吉。象曰、富家大吉、順在位也。

九五、王假有家、勿恤、吉。象曰、王假有家、交相愛也。

上九、有孚、威如、終吉。象曰、威如之吉、反身之謂也。

가인家人은 여자가 곧음이 이롭다.

초9는 집안의 어지러움을 막으면, 후회가 없을 것이다.
62는 이루려는 바 없이 안에서 음식을 맡으면, 바르고 길할 것이다.
93은 가인家人이 준엄하니 지나침을 후회하나 길하다. 부녀자가 희희낙락하면 마침내 궁색할 것이다.
64는 집을 부유하게 하니, 크게 길할 것이다.
95는 왕이 이르러 집을 다스리면, 근심하지 않아도 길할 것이다.
상9는 믿음을 두고 위엄있게 하면, 마침내 길할 것이다.

For the realisation of what is taught in *Jiaren*, or for the regulation of the family, what is most advantageous is that the wife be firm and correct.

1. F9, undivided, shows its subject establishing restrictive regulations in his household. Occasion for repentance will disappear.
2. 62, divided, shows its subject taking nothing on herself, but in her central place attending to the preparation of the food. Through her firm correctness there will be good fortune.
3. 93, undivided, shows its subject treating the members of the household with stern severity. There will be occasion for repentance, there will be peril, but there will also be good fortune. If the wife and children were to be smirking and chattering, in the end there would be occasion for regret.
4. 64, divided, shows its subject enriching the family. There will be great good fortune.
5. 95, undivided, shows the influence of the king extending to his family. There need be no anxiety; there will be good fortune.
6. L9, undivided, shows its subject possessed of sincerity and arrayed in majesty. In the end there will be good fortune.

澤火 ䷥ 睽 (三八)

睽、小事吉。

彖曰、睽、火動而上、澤動而下、二女同居、其志不同行。說而麗乎明、柔進而上行、得中而應乎剛、是以小事吉。天地睽而其事同也、男女睽而其志通也、萬物睽而其事類也、睽之時用大矣哉！

象曰、上火下澤、睽、君子以同而異。

初九、悔亡、喪馬、勿逐、自復、見惡人、无咎。象曰、見惡人、以辟咎也。

九二、遇主于巷、无咎。象曰、遇主于巷、未失道也。

六三、見輿曳、其牛掣、其人天且劓。无初、有終。象曰、見輿曳、位不當也、无初有終、遇剛也。

九四、睽孤、遇元夫、交孚、厲无咎。象曰、交孚无咎、志行也。

六五、悔亡、厥宗噬膚、往何咎？象曰、厥宗噬膚、往有慶也。

上九、睽孤、見豕負塗、載鬼一車、先張之弧、後說之弧、匪寇、婚媾、往遇雨則吉。象曰、遇雨之吉、羣疑亡也。

규睽는 작은 일은 길할 것이다.

초9는 후회가 없으니, 말을 잃고 쫓지 않아도 스스로 돌아오니, 악한 사람을 보아도 허물이 없을 것이다.
92는 주인을 거리에서 만나면 허물이 없을 것이다.
63은 수레가 당겨지고 그 소가 끌리며, 그 사람이 머리 깎이고 또 코가 베여지니, 처음은 없으나 마침은 있을 것이다.
94는 어긋나서 외로워하다가 원래의 장부丈夫를 만나서 미덥게 사귀니, 위태롭지만 허물은 없을 것이다.
65는 후회가 없고 그 종족이 살을 깨무니, 가는 것에 무슨 허물이 있겠는가?
상9는 어긋나서 외로워하다가 진흙을 뒤집어 쓴 것 돼지와 한 수레에 실린 귀신을 본다. 먼저는 활을 당겼다가 뒤에는 활을 벗겨서 도적이 아니라 혼인을 하려는 것이니, 가서 비를 만나면 길할 것이다.

Kui indicates that, notwithstanding the condition of things which it denotes, in small matters there will still be good success.

1. F9, undivided, shows that to its subject occasion for repentance will disappear. He has lost his horses, but let him not seek for them; -they will return of themselves. Should he meet with bad men, he will not err in communicating with them.
2. 92, undivided, shows its subject happening to meet with his lord in a bye-passage. There will be no error.
3. 63, divided, we see one whose carriage is dragged back, while the oxen in it are pushed back, and he is himself subjected to the shaving of his head and the cutting off of his nose. There is no good beginning, but there will be a good end.
4. 94, undivided, shows its subject solitary amidst the prevailing disunion. But he meets with the good man represented by the first line, and they blend their sincere desires together. The position is one of peril, but there will be no mistake.
5. 65, divided, shows that to its subject occasion for repentance will disappear. With his relative and minister he unites closely and readily as if he were biting through a piece of skin. When he goes forward with this help, what error can there be?
6. L9, undivided, shows its subject solitary amidst the prevailing disunion. In the subject of the third line, he seems to see a pig bearing on its back a load of mud, or fancies there is a carriage full of ghosts. He first bends his bow against him, and afterwards unbends it, for he discovers that he is not an assailant to injure, but a near relative. Going forward, he shall meet with genial rain, and there will be good fortune.

山水 ䷦ 蹇 (三九)

蹇、利西南、不利東北、利見大人。貞吉。

象曰、蹇、難也、險在前也、見險而能止、知矣哉！蹇利西南、往得中也、不利東北、其道窮也。利見大人、往有功也、當位貞吉、以正邦也。蹇之時用大矣哉！

象曰、山上有水蹇。君子以、反身修德。

初六、往、蹇、來、譽。象曰、往蹇來譽、宜待也。

六二、王臣蹇蹇、匪躬之故。象曰、王臣蹇蹇、終无尤也。

九三、往、蹇、來、反。象曰、往蹇來反、內喜之也。

六四、往、蹇、來、連。象曰、往蹇來連、位當實也。

九五、大蹇、朋來。象曰、大蹇朋來、以中節也。

上六、往、蹇、來、碩、吉、利見大人。象曰、往蹇來碩、志在內也、利見大人、以從貴也。

건蹇은 서남西南은 이롭고 동북東北은 불리하며 대인大人을 봄이 이로우니, 바르게 하면 길할 것이다.

초6은 가면 험난하고, 오면 명예로울 것이다.
62는 왕과 신하가 험난하고 험난하니, 자신의 이유를 두지 않는다.
93은 가면 험난하고, 오면 반성할 것이다.
64는 가면 험난하고, 오면 어려울 것이다.
95는 크게 어려운데 벗이 올 것이다.
상6은 가면 어렵고 오면 크게 될 것이다. 길하니 대인大人을 봄이 이롭다.

In the state indicated by *Jian* advantage will be found in the south-west, and the contrary in the north-east. It will be advantageous also to meet with the great man. In these circumstances, with firmness and correctness, there will be good fortune.

1. F6, divided, we learn that advance on the part of its subject will lead to greater difficulties, while remaining stationary will afford ground for praise.
2. 62, divided, shows the minister of the king struggling with difficulty on difficulty, and not with a view to his own advantage.
3. 93, undivided, shows its subject advancing, but only to greater difficulties. He remains stationary, and returns to his former associates.
4. 64, divided, shows its subject advancing, but only to greater difficulties. He remains stationary, and unites with the subject of the line above.
5. 95, undivided, shows its subject struggling with the greatest difficulties, while friends are coming to help him.
6. L6, divided, shows its subject going forward, only to increase the difficulties, while his remaining stationary will be productive of great merit. There will be good fortune, and it will be advantageous to meet with the great man.

水雷 ䷧ 解 (四十)

解、利西南、无所往、其來復吉、有攸往、夙、吉。

象曰、解、險以動、動而免乎險、解。解利西南、往得衆也、其來復吉、乃得中也、有攸往夙吉、往有功也。天地解而雷雨作、雷雨 作而百果草木、皆甲坼、解之時大矣哉！

象曰、雷雨作、解、君子以赦過宥罪。

初六、无咎。象曰、剛柔之際、義无咎也。

九二、田獲三狐、得黃失、貞、吉。象曰、九二貞吉、得中道也。

六三、負且乘、致寇至、貞、吝。象曰、負且乘、亦可醜也、自我致戎、又誰咎也？

九四、解而拇、朋至、斯孚。象曰、解而拇、未當位也。

六五、君子維有解、吉、有孚于小人。象曰、君子有解、小人退也。

上六、公用射隼于高墉之上、獲之、无不利。象曰、公用射隼、以解悖也。

해解는 서남西南쪽이 이로우니 갈 곳이 없다. 돌아와서 회복하여 길하니, 갈 곳이 있어 빨리가면 길할 것이다.

초6은 허물이 없을 것이다.
92는 사냥해서 세 마리의 여우를 잡아 누런 화살을 얻으니, 바르게 해야 길할 것이다.
63은 등에 지고 또 탄다. 도적이 이르니, 바르게 해도 궁색할 것이다.
94는 엄지발가락을 풀면 벗이 이르러, 이에 미더울 것이다.
65는 군자가 풀어버리면 길하니, 소인에게 믿음이 있을 것이다.
상6은 공公이 높은 담 위에서 새매를 쏘아 잡으니, 이롭지 않음이 없다.

In the state indicated by *Jie* advantage will be found in the south-west. If no further operations be called for, there will be good fortune in coming back to the old conditions. If some operations be called for, there will be good fortune in the early conducting of them.

1. F6, divided, shows that its subject will commit no error.
2. 92, undivided, shows its subject catch, in hunting, three foxes, and obtain the yellow =golden arrows. With firm correctness there will be good fortune.
3. 63, divided, shows a porter with his burden, yet riding in a carriage. He will only tempt robbers to attack him. However firm and correct he may try to be, there will be cause for regret.
4. 94, undivided, it is said, ' remove your toes. Friends will then come, between you and whom there will be mutual confidence.'
5. 65, divided, shows its subject, the superior man=the ruler, executing his function of removing whatever is injurious to the idea of the hexagram, in which case there will be good fortune, and confidence in him will be shown even by the small men.
6. L6, divided, we see a feudal prince with his bow shooting at a falcon on the top of a high wall, and hitting it. The effect of his action will be in every way advantageous.

澤山 ䷨ 損 (四一)

損、有孚、元吉、无咎、可貞、利有攸往。曷之用？二簋可用享。

彖曰、損、損下益上、其道上行。損而有孚、元吉、无咎可貞利有攸往。曷之用 二簋可用享。二簋應有時、損剛益柔有時、損益盈虛、與時偕行。

象曰、山下有澤、損、君子以懲忿窒欲。

初九、已事、遄往、无咎、酌損之。象曰、已事遄往、尚合志也。

九二、利貞、征、凶、弗損、益之。象曰、九二利貞、中以爲志也。

六三、三人行、則損一人、一人行、則得其友。象曰、一人行、三則疑也。

六四、損其疾、使遄、有喜、无咎。象曰、損其疾、亦可喜也。

六五、或益之十朋之龜、弗克違、元吉。象曰、六五元吉、自上祐也。

上九、弗損益之、无咎、貞吉、利有攸往、得臣、无家。象曰、弗損益之、大得志也。

손損은 믿음이 있으면 크게 길하고 허물이 없어 바르게 될 것이다. 갈 곳이 있어 이로우니 어디에 쓸 것인가? 두 개의 대그릇으로 제사지낼 수 있을 것이다.

초9는 일을 마치면 빨리 가야 허물이 없으니, 참작하여 덜어낸다.
92는 곧음이 이롭고 가면 흉하니, 덜지 않고 보탠다.
63은 세 사람이 가면 곧 한 사람을 덜고, 한 사람이 가면 곧 그 벗을 얻는다.
64는 그 병을 덜되, 빨리하면 기쁨이 있어서 허물이 없을 것이다.
65는 혹 더하면 열무리의 거북도 어기지 않으니, 크게 길할 것이다.
상9는 덜지 말고 더하면 허물이 없으며, 바르게 하여 길하니 가는 것이 이로울 것이다. 신하를 얻으면 집이 없을 것이다.

In what is denoted by *Sun*, if there be sincerity in him employs it, there will be great good fortune:-freedom from error; firmness and correctness that can be maintained; and advantage in every movement that shall be made. In what shall this sincerity in the exercise of Sun be employed? Even in sacrifice two baskets of grain, thought there be nothing else, may be presented.

1. F9, undivided, shows its subject suspending his own affairs, and hurrying away to help the subject of the fourth line. He will commit no error, but let him consider how far he should contribute of what is his for the other.
2. 92, undivided, shows that it will be advantageous for its subject to maintain a firm correctness, and that action on his part will be evil.
   He can give increase to his correlate without taking from himself.
3. 63, divided, shows how of three men walking together, the number is diminished by one; and how one, walking, finds his friend.
4. 64, divided, shows its subject diminishing the ailment under which he labours by making the subject of the first line hasten to his help, and make him glad. There will be no error.
5. 65, divided, shows parties adding to the stores of its subject ten pairs of tortoise shells, and accepting no refusal. There will be great good fortune.
6. L9, undivided, shows its subject giving increase to others without taking from himself. There will be no error. With firm correctness there will be good fortune. There will be advantage in every movement that shall be made. He will find ministers more than can be counted by their clans.

雷風 ䷩ 益 (四二)

益、利有攸往、利涉大川。

彖曰、益、損上益下、民說无疆、自上下下、其道大光。利有攸往、中正有慶、利涉大川、木道乃行。益、動而巽、日進无疆、天施地生、其益、无方。凡益之道、與時偕行。

象曰、風雷、益、君子以見善則遷、有過則改。

初九、利用爲大作、元吉、无咎。象曰、元吉无咎、下不厚事也。

六二、或益之十朋之、龜、弗克違、永貞、吉、王用享于帝、吉。象曰、或益之、自外來也。

六三、益之用凶事、无咎、有孚中行、告公用圭。象曰、益用凶事、固有之也。

六四、中行、告公從、利用爲依、遷國。象曰、告公從、以益志也。

九五、有孚惠心、勿問、元吉、有孚、惠我德。象曰、有孚惠心、勿問之矣、惠我德、大得志也。

上九、莫益之、或擊之、立心勿恒、凶。象曰、莫益之、偏辭也、或擊之、自外來也。

익益은 갈 바 있어 이롭고, 큰 내를 건너는 것이 이롭다.

초9는 큰 일을 하는 것이 이로우니, 크게 길하여 허물이 없을 것이다.
62는 혹 더하면 열 무리의 거북도 어기지 못한다. 영구히 바르게 하면 길하니, 왕이 상제께 제사지내면 길할 것이다.
63은 더하니 흉한 일에 쓰면 허물이 없다 믿음을 두고 중도中道를 행하여야 공公에 고하여 규圭를 쓸 것이다.
64는 중도中道로 행하여 공公에게 고하면 순종할 것이다. 이로써 의지하여 나라를 옮기는 것이 이롭다.
95는 믿음을 두어 마음을 은혜롭게 하는 것이다. 묻지 않아도 크게 길하니, 믿음을 두어 나의 덕을 은혜롭게 여길 것이다.
상9는 더해주지 않는 것이다. 혹 치기도 하여 마음을 세우는 것이 일정하지 않으니 흉하다.

Yi indicates that in the state which it denotes there will be advantage in every movement which shall be undertaken, that it will be advantageous even to cross the great stream.

1. F9, undivided, shows that it will be advantageous for its subject in his position to make a great movement. If it be greatly fortunate, no blame will be imputed to him.
2. 62, divided, shows parties adding to the stores of its subject ten pairs of tortoise shells whose oracles cannot be opposed. Let him persevere in being firm and correct, and there will be good fortune. Let the king,having the virtues thus distinguished, employ them in presenting his offerings to God, and there will be good fortune.
3. 63, divided, shows increase given to its subject by means of what is evil, so that he shall be led to good, and be without blame. Let him be sincere and pursue the path of the Mean, so shall he secure the recognition of the ruler, like an officer who announces himself to his prince by the symbol of his rank.
4. 64, divided, shows its subject pursuing the due course. His advice to his prince is followed. He can with advantage be relied on in such a movement as that of removing the capital.
5. 95, undivided, shows its subject with sincere heart seeking to benefit all below. There need be no question about it; the result will be great good fortune. All below will with sincere heart acknowledge his goodness.
6. L9, undivided, we see one to whose increase none will contribute, while many will seek to assail him he observes no regular rule in the ordering of his heart. There will be evil.

天澤 ䷪ 夬 四三

夬、揚于王庭、孚號有厲、告自邑、不利卽戎、利有攸往。

象曰、夬、決也、剛決柔也、健而說、決而和。揚于王庭、柔乘五剛也、孚號有厲、其危乃光也、告自邑不利卽戎、所尙乃窮也、利有攸往、剛長乃終也。

象曰、澤上於天、夬、君子以施祿及下、居德則忌。

初九、壯于前趾、往、不勝、爲咎。象曰、不勝而往、咎也。

九二、惕號、莫夜、有戎、勿恤。象曰、有戎勿恤、得中道也。

九三、壯于頄、有凶、獨行遇雨、君子、夬夬。若濡有慍、无咎。

象曰、君子夬夬、終无咎也。

九四、臀无膚、其行次且、牽羊、悔亡、聞言、不信。象曰、其行次且、位不當也、聞言不信、聰不明也。

九五、莧陸夬夬、中行无咎。象曰、中行无咎、中未光也。

上六、无號、終有凶。象曰、无號之凶、終不可長也。

쾌夬는 왕의 뜰(조정)에서 드날리는 것이니 미더운 부르짖음에 위태로움이 있다. 읍邑으로부터 고할 것이요, 병력을 바로 동원하면 불리하니, 가는 바를 있으면 이로울 것이다.

초9는 앞발꿈치에 힘을 주니, 가면 이기지 못하고 허물이 될 것이다.
92는 두렵게 부르짖으나, 밤에 병란이 있더라도 근심하지 말라.
93은 광대뼈가 튀어나와 흉함이 있으며, 홀로 행하여 비를 만나 젖으니, 군자는 결단할 것을 결단한다. 비에 젖어서 성은 나지만 허물은 없을 것이다.
94는 볼기에 살이 없으며 그 행함을 머뭇거리니 양을 끌면 후회가 없을 것이다. 말을 듣더라도 믿지 않을 것이다.
95는 부드러운 풀처럼 쉽게 결단할 것을 결단하면, 가운데서 행함에 허물이 없을 것이다.
상6은 호소할 데가 없으니, 마침내 흉함이 있을 것이다.

Guai requires in him who would fulfil its meaning the exhibition of the culprit's guilt in the royal court, and a sincere and earnest appeal for sympathy and support, with a consciousness of the peril involved in cutting off the criminal. He should also make announcement in his own city, and show that it will not be well to have recourse at once to arms. In this way there will be advantage in whatever he shall go forward to.

1. F9, undivided, shows its subject in the pride of strength advancing with his toes. He goes forward, but will not succeed. There will be ground for blame.
2. 92, undivided, shows its subject full of apprehension and appealing for sympathy and help. Late at night hostile measures may be taken against him, but he need not be anxious about them.
3. 93, undivided, shows its subject about to advance with strong and determined looks. There will be evil. But the superior man, bent on cutting off the criminal, will walk alone and encounter the rain, till he be hated by his proper associates as if he were contaminated by the others. In the end there will be no blame against him.
4. 94, undivided, shows one from whose buttocks the skin has been stripped, and who walks slowly and with difficulty. If he could act like a sheep led after its companions, occasion for repentance would disappear. But though he hear these words, he will not believe them.
5. 95, undivided, shows the small men like a bed of purslain, which ought to be uprooted with the utmost determination. The subject of the line having such determination, his action, in harmony with his central position, will lead to no error or blame.
6. L6, divided, shows its subject without any helpers on whom to call. His end will be evil.

風天 ䷫ 姤 (四四)

姤、女壯、勿用取女。

象曰、姤、遇也、柔遇剛也。勿用取女、不可與長也。天地相遇、品物咸章也、剛遇中正、天下大行也。姤之時義大矣哉！

象曰、天下有風、姤、后以施命誥四方。

初六、繫于金柅、貞吉、有攸往、見凶、羸豕孚蹢躅。象曰、繫于金柅、柔道牽也。

九二、包有魚、无咎、不利賓。象曰、包有魚、義不及賓也。

九三、臀无膚、其行、次且、厲、无大咎。象曰、其行次且、行未牽也。

九四、包无魚、起凶。象曰、无魚之凶、遠民也。

九五、以杞包瓜、含章、有隕自天。象曰、九五含章、中正也、有隕自天、志不舍命也。

上九、姤其角、吝、无咎。象曰、姤其角、上窮、吝也。

구姤는 여자가 씩씩한 것이니, 여자를 취하지 말아야 한다.

초6은 쇠말뚝에 매면 바르게 함이 길하고, 가는 바가 있으면 흉함을 볼 것이니, 암돼지가 가벼이 날뛴다.

92는 부엌에 물고기가 있으면 허물이 없을 것이니, 손님에는 이롭지 않다.

93은 볼기에 살이 없으며 그 행함을 비틀거리니, 위태롭기는 하나 큰 허물이 없을 것이다.

94는 부엌에 물고기가 없으니 일어남이 흉할 것이다.

95는 구기자와 호롱박으로써 아름다움을 머금었으나, 하늘로부터 떨어짐이 있을 것이다.

상9는 그 뿔을 만나는 것이니, 궁색하나 허물은 없을 것이다.

Gou shows a female who is bold and strong. It will not be good to marry such a female.

1. F6, divided, shows how its subject should be kept like a carriage tied and fastened to a metal drag, in which case with firm correctness there will be good fortune. But if he move in any direction, evil will appear. He will be like a lean pig, which is sure to keep jumping about.
2. 92, undivided, shows its subject with a wallet of fish. There will be no error. But it will not be well to let the subject of the first line go forward to the guests.
3. 93, undivided, shows onc from whose buttocks the skin has been stripped so that he walks with difficulty. The position is perilous, but there will be no great error.
4. 94, undivided, shows its subject with his wallet, but no fish in it. This will give rise to evil.
5. 95, undivided, shows its subject as a medlar tree over-spreading the gourd beneath it. If he keep his brilliant qualities concealed, a good issue will descend as from Heaven.
6. L9, undivided, shows its subject receiving others on his horns. There will be occasion for regret, but there will be no error.

地澤 ䷬ 萃 四五

萃、亨王假有廟、利見大人、亨、利貞、用大牲、吉、利有攸往。

彖曰、萃、聚也、順以說、剛中而應、故聚也。王假有廟、致孝享也、利見大人亨、聚以正也、用大牲吉利有攸往、順天命也。觀其所聚而天地萬物之情、可見矣！

象曰、澤上於地、萃、君子以除戎器、戒不虞。

初六、有孚、不終、乃亂乃萃、若號、一握爲笑、勿恤、往、无咎。

象曰、乃亂乃萃、其志亂也。

六二、引、吉、无咎、孚乃利用禴。象曰、引吉无咎、中未變也。

六三、萃如嗟如、无攸利、往、无咎、小吝。象曰、往无咎、上巽也。

九四、大吉、无咎。象曰、大吉无咎、位不當也。

九五、萃有位、无咎、匪孚、元永貞、悔亡。象曰、萃有位、志未光也。

上六、齎咨涕洟、无咎。象曰、齎咨涕洟、未安上也。

췌萃는 형통하니 왕이 사당에 이르고 대인을 봄이 이롭다. 형통하니 바르게 함이 이롭다. 큰 희생을 쓰는 것이 길하니 가는 바가 있음이 이롭다.

초6은 믿음이 있으나 끝까지 지속하지 못하면 어지러워졌다가 모였다 할 것이니, 만약 부르짖으면 한번 손잡고 웃게 될 것이니, 근심하지 말고 가면 허물이 없을 것이다.
62는 이끌면 길하여 허물이 없을 것이니, 믿어서 간략히 제사올리는 것이 이롭다.
63은 모이는 듯 탄식하는 듯하다. 이로운 바가 없으니, 가면 허물이 없겠지만 조금 궁색할 것이다.
94는 크게 길하여 허물이 없을 것이다.
95는 모이는데 자리가 있고 허물이 없으나, 믿지 않아서 크게 오래도록 바르게 하면 후회가 없을 것이다.
상6은 탄식하며 눈물을 흘리니, 허물이 없을 것이다.

In the state denoted by *Cui*, the king will repair to his ancestral temple. It will be advantageous also to meet with the great man; and then there will progress and success, though the advantage must come through firm correctness. The use of great victims will conduce to good fortune; and in whatever direction movement is made, it will be advantageous.

1. F6, divided, shows its subject with a sincere desire for union, but unable to carry it out, so that disorder is brought into the sphere of his union. If he cry out for help to his proper correlate, all at once his tears will give place to smiles. He need not mind the temporary difficulty; as he goes forward, there will be no error.
2. 62, divided, shows its subject led forward by his correlate. There will be good fortune, and freedom from error. There is entire sincerity, and in that case even the small offerings of the vernal sacrifice are acceptable.
3. 63, divided, shows its subject striving after union and seeming to sigh, yet nowhere finding any advantage. If he go forward, he will not err, though there may be some small cause for regret.
4. 94, undivided, shows its subject in such a state that, if he be greatly fortunate, he will receive no blame.
5. 95, undivided, shows the union of all under its subject in the place of dignity. There will be no error. If any do not have confidence in him, let him see to it that his virtue be great, longcontinued, and firmly correct, and all occasion for repentance will disappear.
6. L6, divided, shows its subject sighing and weeping ; but there will be no error.

風地 ䷭ 升 四六

升、元亨、用見大人、勿恤、南征、吉。

象曰、柔以時升、巽而順、剛中而應、是以大亨。用見大人、勿恤、有慶也、南征吉、志行也。

象曰、地中生木、升、君子以順德、積小以高大。

初六、允升、大吉。象曰、允升大吉、上合志也。

九二、孚乃利用禴、无咎。象曰、九二之孚、有喜也。

九三、升虛邑。象曰、升虛邑、无所疑也。

六四、王用亨于岐山、吉、无咎。象曰、王用亨于岐山、順事也。

六五、貞、吉、升階。象曰、貞吉升階、大得志也。

上六、冥升、利于不息之貞。象曰、冥升在上、消不富也。

승升은 크게 형통하되 대인을 만나야 근심하지 않을 것이다. 남쪽으로 가면 길할 것이다.

초6은 마땅히 올라야 하니, 크게 길할 것이다.
92는 믿어서 간략하게 제사지냄이 이로우니, 허물이 없을 것이다.
93은 빈 읍邑에 오르는 것이다.
64는 왕이 기산岐山에서 제사를 지내면 길하고 허물이 없을 것이다.
65는 바르게 해서 길하니, 섬돌에 오를 것이다.
상6은 어두워도 오르는 것이니, 쉬지 않고 바르게 함이 이롭다.

Sheng indicates that under its conditions there will be great progress and success. Seeking by the qualities implied in it to meet with the great man, its subject need have no anxiety. Advance to the south will be fortunate.

1. F6, divided, shows its subject advancing upwards with the welcome of those above him. There will be great good fortune.
2. 92, undivided, shows its subject with that sincerity which will make even the small offerings of the vernal sacrifice acceptable. There will be no error.
3. 93, undivided, shows its subject ascending upwards as into an empty city.
4. 64, divided, shows its subject employed by the king to present his offerings on mount Khi. There will be good fortune ; there will be no mistake.
5. 65, divided, shows its subject firmly correct, and therefore enjoying good fortune. He ascends the stairs with all due ceremony.
6. L6, divided, shows its subject advancing upwards blindly. Advantage will be found in a ceaseless maintenance of firm correctness.

水澤 困 ㊼

困、亨、貞、大人、吉、无咎、有言、不信。

象曰、困、剛揜也。險以說、困而不失其所亨、其唯君子乎！貞大人吉、以剛中也、有言不信、尚口乃窮也。

象曰、澤无水、困、君子以致命遂志。

初六、臀困于株木、入于幽谷、三歲、不覿。象曰、入于幽谷、幽不明也。

九二、困于酒食、朱紱方來、利用享祀、征凶、无咎。象曰、困于酒食、中有慶也。

六三、困于石、據于蒺蔾、入于其宮、不見其妻、凶。象曰、據于蒺蔾、乘剛也、入于其宮、不見其妻、不祥也。

九四、來徐徐、困于金車、吝、有終。象曰、來徐徐、志在下也、雖不當位、有與也。

九五、劓刖、困于赤紱、乃徐有說、利用祭祀。象曰、劓刖、志未得也、乃徐有說、以中直也、利用祭祀、受福也。

上六、困于葛藟、于臲卼、曰動悔、有悔、征、吉。象曰、困于葛藟、未當也、動悔有悔、吉行也。

곤困은 형통하고 바르며, 대인代人이라야 길하고 허물이 없으니, 말이 있어도 믿지 않을 것이다.

초6은 엉덩이가 나무뿌리에 걸려 곤궁함이다. 어두운 골짜기에 들어가서 삼년이 되어도 보지 못한다.

92는 마시고 먹는데 피곤하며, 남방의 사물도 곧 찾아 오니, 제사를 올리는 것이 이롭다. 가면 흉할 것이나 허물은 없다.

63은 돌에 걸려 곤궁하며 가시덤불에 의지하는 것이다. 그 집에 들어가더라도 그 처를 보지 못하니 흉하다.

94는 오는 것이 느린 것은 쇠수레가 곤궁하기 때문이니, 궁색하나 마침은 있을 것이다.

95는 코를 베고 발꿈치를 베면 남쪽 지방에서 곤궁하나, 서서히 하면 기쁨이 있을 것이다. 제사를 지냄이 이롭다

상6은 칡넝쿨과 위태로운 데에 곤궁함이니, 움직여서 후회한다고 말한다. 후회가 있어서 가면 길할 것이다.

In the condition denoted by *Kun* there may yet be progress and success. For the firm and correct, the really great man, there will be good fortune. He will fall into no error. If he make speeches, his words cannot be made good.

1. F6, divided, shows its subject with bare buttocks straitened under the stump of a tree. He enters a dark valley, and for three years has no prospect of deliverance.
2. 92, undivided, shows its subject straitened amidst his wine and viands. There come to him anon the red knee covers of the ruler. It will be well for him to maintain his sincerity as in sacrificing. Active operations on his part will lead to evil, but he will be free from blame.
3. 63, divided, shows its subject straitened before a frowning rock. He lays hold of thorns. He enters his palace, and does not see his wife. There will be evil.
4. 94, undivided, shows its subject proceeding very slowly to help the subject of the first line, who is straitened by the carriage adorned with metal in front of him. There will be occasion for regret, but the end will be good.
5. 95, undivided, shows its subject with his nose and feet cut off. He is straitened by his ministers in their scarlet aprons. He is leisurely in his movements, however, and is satisfied. It will be well for him to be as sincere as in sacrificing to spiritual beings.
6. L6, divided, shows its subject straitened, as if bound with creepers; or in a high and dangerous position, and saying to himself. 'If I move, I shall repent it.' If he do repent of formererrors, there will be good fortune in his going forward.

風水 ䷯ 井 (四八)

井、改邑、不改井、无喪无得、往來井井、汔至亦未繘井、羸其瓶、凶。

象曰、巽乎水而上水井、井、養而不窮也。改邑不改井、乃以剛中也、汔至亦未繘井、未有功也、羸其瓶、是以凶也。

象曰、木上有水、井、君子以勞民勸相。

初六、井泥不食、舊井、无禽。象曰、井泥不食、下也、舊井无禽、時舍也。

九二、井谷、射鮒、甕敝漏。象曰、井谷射鮒、无與也。

九三、井渫不食、爲我心惻、可用汲、王明、並受其福。象曰、井渫不食、行惻也、求王明、受福也。

六四、井甃、无咎。象曰、井甃无咎、脩井也。

九五、井冽寒泉食。象曰、寒泉之食、中正也。

上六、井收勿幕、有孚、元吉。象曰、元吉在上、大成也。

정井은 읍邑은 고쳐도 우물은 고치지 못하니, 잃는 것도 없고 얻는 것도 없다. 가고 오는 사람이 우물을 쓰지만 거의 이르러 우물물을 긷지 못하니, 그 두레박이 걸리면 흉할 것이다.

초6은 우물이 진흙탕이라 먹지 못하니, 오래된 우물에 새가 없다.
92는 우물이 골짜기처럼 물을 흘려보내니, 독이 깨져서 물이 샌다.
93은 우물이 깨끗이 치워졌는데 먹지 못해서 나의 마음이 슬프다. 물을 퍼서 쓸만하니 왕이 밝으면 아울러 그 복을 받을 것이다.
64는 우물을 치면 허물이 없을 것이다.
95는 우물이 맑고 차서 찬 샘물을 먹는다.
상6은 우물의 물을 거두어 쓰고 덮지 않으니 믿음이 있어 크게 길할 것이다.

Looking at *Jing*, we think of how the site of a town may be changed, while the fashion of its wells undergoes no change. The water of a well never disappears and never receives any great increase, and those who come and those who go can draw and enjoy the benefit. If the drawing have nearly been accomplished, but, before the rope has quite reached the water, the bucket is broken, this is evil.

1. F6, divided, shows a well so muddy that men will not drink of it; or an old well to which neither birds nor other creatures resort.
2. 92, undivided, shows a well from which by a hole the water escapes and flows away to the shrimps and such small creatures among the grass, or one the water of which leaks away from a broken basket.
3. 93, undivided, shows a well, which has been cleared out, but is not used. Our hearts are sorry for this, for the water might be drawn out and used. If the king were only intelligent, both he and we might receive the benefit of it.
4. 64, divided, shows a well, the lining of which is well laid. There will be no error.
5. 95, undivided, shows a clear, limpid well, the waters from whose cold spring are freely drunk.
6. L6, divided, shows the water from the well brought to the top, which is not allowed to be covered. This suggests the idea of sincerity. There will be great good fortune.

火澤 ䷰ 革 ㊾

革、己日、乃孚、元亨、利貞、悔亡。

象曰、革、水火相息、二女同居、其志不相得、曰革。己日乃孚、革而信之、文明以說、大亨以正、革而當、其悔乃亡。天地革而四時成、湯武革命、順乎天而應乎人、革之時大矣哉！

象曰、澤中有火革、君子以治歷明時。

初九、鞏用黃牛之革。象曰、鞏用黃牛、不可以有爲也。

六二、己日、乃革之、征、吉、无咎。象曰、己日革之、行有嘉也。

九三、征、凶、貞厲、革言、三就、有孚。象曰、革言三就、又何之矣！

九四、悔亡、有孚、改命、吉。象曰、改命之吉、信志也。

九五、大人、虎變、未占、有孚。象曰、大人虎變、其文、炳也。

上六、君子豹變、小人、革面、征、凶、居貞、吉。象曰、君子豹變、其文、蔚也、小人革面、順以從君也。

혁革은 시일이 지나야 이에 믿을 것이니, 크게 형통하고 바르게 함이 이로워서 후회가 없다.

초9는 굳게 하여 황소의 가죽을 쓸 것이다.
62는 시일이 지나야 이에 바꿀 것이니, 가면 길하여 허물이 없을 것이다.
93은 정벌하면 흉하니 바르더라도 위태로울 것이니다. 바꾼다는 말이 세 번 성취되니 믿음이 있다.
94는 후회가 없으니, 믿음이 있으면 명을 바꿔서 길할 것이다.
95는 대인이 호랑이로 변하는 것이니, 점치기 전에 믿음이 있다.
상6은 군자가 표범으로 변하고 소인은 낯을 고치니, 가면 흉하고 거처하면 바르기에 길할 것이다.

What takes place as indicated by *Ge* is believed in only after it has been accomplished. There will be great progress and success. Advantage will come from being firm and correct. In that case occasion for repentance will disappear.

1. F9, undivided, shows its subject as if he were bound with the skin of a yellow ox.
2. 62, divided, shows its subject making his changes after some time has passed. Action taken will be fortunate. There will be no error.
3. 93, undivided, shows that action taken by its subject will be evil. Though he be firm and correct, his position is perilous. If the change he contemplates have been three times fully discussed, he will be believed in.
4. 94, undivided, shows occasion for repentance disappearing from its subject. Let him be believed in ; and though he change existing ordinances, there will be good fortune.
5. 95, undivided, shows the great man producing his changes as the tiger does when he changes his stripes. Before he divines and proceeds to action, faith has been reposed in him.
6. L6, divided, shows the superior man producing his changes as the leopard does when he changes his spots, while small men change their faces and show their obedience. To go forward now would lead to evil, but there will be good fortune in abiding firm and correct.

風火 ䷱ 鼎 五十

鼎、元吉亨。

象曰、鼎、象也。以木巽火亨飪也。聖人、亨、以享上帝、而大亨、以養聖賢。巽而耳目、聰明、柔進而上行、得中而應乎剛、是以元亨。

象曰、木上有火、鼎、君子以正位、凝命。

初六、鼎、顚趾、利出否、得妾、以其子无咎。象曰、鼎顚趾、未悖也、利出否、以從貴也。

九二、鼎有實、我仇有疾、不我能卽、吉。象曰、鼎有實、愼所之也、我仇有疾、終无尤也。

九三、鼎耳革、其行、塞、雉膏、不食、方雨、虧悔終吉。象曰、鼎耳革、失其義也。

九四、鼎、折足、覆公餗、其形、渥、凶。象曰、覆公餗、信如何也!

六五、鼎黃耳金鉉、利貞。象曰、鼎黃耳、中以爲實也。

上九、鼎玉鉉、大吉、无不利。象曰、玉鉉在上、剛柔、節也。

정鼎은 크게 길하여 형통할 것이다.

초6은 솥이 발꿈치에 엎어졌으나, 비색한 것을 내놓는 것이 이롭다. 첩을 얻으면 그 자식으로써 허물이 없을 것이다.

92는 솥이 실하게 차 있으니 내짝에 병이 있어 내게 올 수 없으면 길할 것이다.

93은 솥귀를 고치려 하다가 막히니 꿩고기를 먹지 못한다. 바야흐로 비가 오면, 후회가 사그라지고 마침내 길하게 될 것이다.

94는 솥이 다리가 부러져서 여러 음식을 엎어서 그 몸이 젖으니, 흉하다.

65는 솥이 누런 귀에 금고리이니, 곧게 함이 이롭다.

상9는 솥의 옥 고리이니, 크게 길해서 이롭지 않음이 없다.

Ding gives the intimation of great progress and success.

1. F6, divided, shows the caldron overthrown and its feet turned up. But there will be advantage in its getting rid of what was bad in it. Or it shows us the concubine whose position is improved by means of her son. There will be no error.
2. 92, undivided, shows the caldron with the things to be cooked in it. If its subject can say, 'My enemy dislikes me, but he cannot approach me, there will be good fortune.
3. 93, undivided, shows the caldron with the places of its ears changed. The progress of its subject is thus stopped. The fat flesh of the pheasant which is in the caldron will not be eaten. But the genial rain will come, and the grounds for repentance will disappear. There will be good fortune in the end.
4. 94, undivided, shows the caldron with its feet broken; and its contents, designed for the ruler's use, overturned and spilt. Its subject will be made to blush for shame. There will be evil.
5. 65, divided, shows the caldron with yellow ears and rings of metal in them. There will be advantage through being firm and correct.
6. L9, undivided, shows the caldron with rings of jade. There will be great good fortune, and all action taken will be in every way advantageous.

雷重 震 (五一)

震、亨。震來、虩虩、笑言、啞啞、震驚百里、不喪匕鬯。

象曰、震、亨。震來虩虩、恐致福也、笑言啞啞、後有則也。震驚百里、驚遠而懼邇也、出可以守宗廟社稷、以爲祭主也。

象曰、洊雷震、君子以、恐懼脩省。

初九、震來虩虩、後、笑言啞啞、吉。象曰、震來虩虩、恐致福也、笑言啞啞、後有則也。

六二、震來厲、億喪貝、躋于九陵、勿逐、七日得。象曰、震來厲、乘剛也。

六三、震蘇蘇、震行、无眚。象曰、震蘇蘇、位不當也。

九四、震、遂泥。象曰、震遂泥、未光也。

六五、震、往來、厲、億、无喪有事。象曰、震往來厲、危行也、其事在中、大无喪也。

上六、震、索索、視矍矍、征、凶、震不于其躬、于其鄰、无咎、婚媾有言。象曰、震索索、中未得也、雖凶无咎、畏鄰戒也。

진震은 형통하니 천둥이 칠 때 놀라서 떨면 웃는 소리가 깔깔거리니, 천둥이 백리 밖까지 놀라게 해도 종묘제사를 잃지 않는다.

초9는 천둥이 칠 때 놀라서 떨면 깔깔거리며 웃는 소리가 날 것이니, 길하다.

62는 천둥이 치니 위태롭다. 재물을 잃고 구릉을 넘어가나 쫓지 않아도 칠일만에 잡을 것이다.

63은 우뢰에 두려워 떠니, 두려워하면서 가면 재앙이 없을 것이다.

94는 우뢰가 진흙에 빠지는 것이다.

65는 우뢰가 가고 옴에 두려워하니, 잃지는 않고 일이 있다.

상6은 두려워 불안하여 눈을 두리번거리니, 가면 흉하다. 두려워함이 그 몸에 있지 않고 그 이웃에 있으면 허물이 없을 것이니, 혼인은 말이 있을 것이다.

Zhen gives the intimation of ease and development. When the time of movement which it indicates comes, the subject of the hexagram will be found looking out with apprehension, and yet smiling and talking cheerfully. When the movement like a crash of thunder terrifies all within a hundred li, he will be like the sincere worshipper who is not startled into letting go his ladle and cup of sacrificial spirits.

1. F9, undivided, shows its subject, when the movement approaches, looking out and around with apprehension, and afterwards smiling and talking cheerfully. There will be good fortune.
2. 62, divided, shows its subject, when the movement approaches, in a position of peril. He judges it better to let go the articles in his possession, and to ascend a very lofty height. There is no occasion for him to pursue after the things he has let go; in seven days he will find them.
3. 63, divided, shows its subject distraught amid the startling movements going on. If those movements excite him to right action, there will be no mistake.
4. 94, undivided, shows its subject, amid the startling movements, supinely sinking deeper in the mud.
5. 65, divided, shows its subject going and coming amidst the startling movements of the time, and always in peril; but perhaps he will not incur loss, and find business which he can accomplish.
6. L6, divided, shows its subject, amidst the startling movements of the time, in breathless dismay and looking round him with trembling apprehension. If he take action, there will be evil. If, whild the startling movements have not reached his own person and his neighbourhood, he were to take precautions, there would be no error, though his relatives might still speak against him.

山重 ䷳ 艮 ㊾

艮　艮其背、不獲其身、行其庭、不見其人。无咎。

彖曰、艮、止也。時止則止、時行則行、動靜不失其時、其道光明。艮其止、止其所也。上下敵應、不相與也、是以不獲其身行其庭不見其人无咎也。

象曰、兼山、艮、君子以、思不出其位。

初六、艮其趾、无咎、利永貞。象曰、艮其趾、未失正也。

六二、艮其腓、不拯其隨、其心不快。象曰、不拯其隨、未退聽也。

九三、艮其限、列其夤、厲薰心。象曰、艮其限、危薰心也。

六四、艮其身、无咎。象曰、艮其身、止諸躬也。

六五、艮其輔、言有序、悔亡。象曰、艮其輔、以中、正也。

上九、敦艮、吉。象曰、敦艮之吉、以厚終也。

그 등에 그치면 그 몸을 얻지 못하며 그 뜰에 거닐어도 그 사람을 보지 못하니, 허물이 없을 것이다.

초6은 그 발꿈치에 그쳐서 허물이 없으니, 길이 바르게 함이 이롭다.
62는 그 장딴지에 그치는 것이니, 발꿈치를 들지 못해서, 그 마음이 유쾌하지 않다.
93은 그 허리에 그치는 것이니, 그 등이 찢어져서 위태하니, 마음이 찌는 듯 하다.
64는 그 몸에 그치는 것이니, 허물이 없다.
65는 그 뺨에 그치는 것이니, 말이 차례가 있어서 후회가 없다.
상9는 도타웁게 그치는 것이니, 길하다.

When one's resting is like that of the back, and he loses all consciousness of self; when he walks in his courtyard, and does not see any of the persons in it, - there will be no error.

1. F6, divided, shows its subject keeping his toes at rest. There will be no error ; but it will be advantageous for him to be persistently firm and correct.
2. 62, divided, shows its subject keeping the calves of his legs at rest. he cannot help the subject of the line above whom he follows, and is dissatisfied in his mind.
3. 93, undivided, shows its subject keeping his loins at rest, and separating the ribs from the body blows with suppressed excitement.
4. 64, divided, shows its subject keeping his trunk at rest. there will be no error.
5. 65, divided, shows its subject keeping his jawbones at rest, so that his words are all orderly. occasion for repentance will disappear.
6. L9, undivided, shows its subject devotedly maintaining his restfulness. there will be good fortune.

山風 ䷴ 漸 ㊈

漸、女歸吉、利貞。
象曰、漸之進也、女歸、吉也。進得位、往有功也、進以正、可以正邦也。其位、剛得中也、止而巽、動不窮也。
象曰、山上有木、漸、君子以、居賢德、善俗。
初六、鴻漸于干、小子厲、有言、无咎。象曰、小子之厲、義无咎也。
六二、鴻漸于磐、飮食、衎衎、吉。象曰、飮食衎衎、不素飽也。
九三、鴻漸于陸、夫征、不復、婦孕、不育、凶、利禦寇。象曰、夫征不復、離羣、醜也、婦孕不育、失其道也、利用禦寇、順相保也。
六四、鴻漸于木、或得其桷、无咎。象曰、或得其桷、順以巽也。
九五、鴻漸于陵、婦三歲、不孕、終莫之勝、吉。象曰、終莫之勝吉、得所願也。
上九、鴻漸于陸、其羽可用爲儀、吉。象曰、其羽可用爲儀吉、不可亂也。

점漸은 여자가 시집가는 것이 길하니, 바르게 하는 것이 이롭다.

초6은 기러기가 물가에 나아가는 것이니, 소자小子가 위태하여 말해도 허물이 없을 것이다.

62는 기러기가 반석에 나아가는 것이니, 마시고 먹는 것이 즐겁고 길하다.

93은 기러기가 언덕에 나아가는 것이니, 지아비가 가면 돌아오지 못하고 지어미가 잉태하여도 기르지 못하니 흉하다. 도적을 막는 것이 이롭다.

64는 기러기가 나무에 날아가는 것이니, 혹 그 가지를 얻으면 허물이 없을 것이다.

95는 기러기가 언덕으로 날아가는 것이니, 지어미가 삼년을 애를 배지 못하여 마침내 이기지 못하니, 길할 것이다.

상9는 기러기가 꼭대기로 날아가는 것이니, 그 깃으로써 의표儀表를 삼을만 하니, 길하다.

Jian suggests to us the marriage of a young lady, and the good fortune attending it. There will be advantage in being firm and correct.

1. F6, divided, shows the wild geese gradually approaching the shore. A young officer in similar circumstances will be in a position of danger, and be spoken against; but there will be no error.
2. 62, divided, shows the geese gradually approaching the large rocks, where they eat and drink joyfully and at ease. There will be good fortune.
3. 93, undivided, shows them gradually advanced to the dry plains. It suggests also the idea of a husband who goes on an expedition from which he does not return, and of a wife who is pregnant, but will not nourish her child. There will be evil. The case symbolised might be advantageous in resisting plunderers.
4. 64, divided, shows the geese gradually advanced to the trees. They may light on the flat branches. There will be no error.
5. 95, undivided, shows the geese gradually advanced to the high mound. It suggests the idea of a wife who for three years dose not become pregnant; but in the end the natural issue cannot be prevented. There will be good fortune.
6. L9, undivided, shows the geese gradually advanced to the large heights beyond. Their feathers can be used us ornaments. There will be good fortune.

澤雷 歸妹 (五四)

歸妹、征、凶、无攸利。

象曰、歸妹、天地之大義也。天地不交而萬物、不興、歸妹、人之終始也。說以動、所歸妹也、征凶、位不當也、无攸利、柔乘剛也。

象曰、澤上有雷、歸妹、君子以、永終、知敝。

初九、歸妹以娣、跛能履、征、吉。象曰、歸妹以娣、以恒也、跛能履吉、相承也。

九二、眇能視、利幽人之貞。象曰、利幽人之貞、未變常也。

六三、歸妹以須、反歸以娣。象曰、歸妹以須、未當也。

九四、歸妹愆期、遲歸有時。象曰、愆期之志、有待而行也。

六五、帝乙歸妹、其君之袂、不如其娣之袂良、月幾望、吉。象曰、帝乙歸妹不如其娣之袂良也、其位在中、以貴行也。

上六、女承筐无實、士刲羊无血。无攸利。象曰、上六无實、承虛筐也。

귀매歸妹는 가면 흉하니 이로울 바가 없다.

초9는 누이동생을 시집보내는데 첩으로써 하니, 절름발이도 걷는 격이다. 가면 길할 것이다.

92는 소경이 볼 수 있으니, 숨어사는 사람은 바르게 함이 이롭다.

63은 누이동생을 시집보내는데 기다리니, 돌아가서 제첩으로써 시집간다.

94는 누이동생을 시집보내는데 시기를 놓치는 것이니, 시집을 늦게 가는 데도 때가 있다.

65는 제을帝乙이 누이동생을 시집보내는데, 그 주인의 소매가 그 동생의 좋은 소매만 같지 못하니, 달이 거의 보름이면 길할 것이다.

상6은 여자가 광주리를 이는데 내용이 없다. 남자가 양을 찔러서 피가 없으니, 이로운 것이 없다.

Guimei Mei indicates that under the conditions which it denotes action will be evil, and in no wise advantageous.

1. F9, undivided, shows the younger sister married off in a position ancillary to the real wife. It suggests the idea of a person lame on one leg who yet manages to tramp along. Going forward will be fortunate.
2. 92, undivided, shows her blind of one eye, and yet able to see. There will be advantage in her maintaining the firm correctness of a solitary widow.
3. 63, divided, shows the younger sister who was to be married off in a mean position. She returns and accepts an ancillary position.
4. 94, undivided, shows the younger sister who is to be married off protracting the time. She may be late in being married, but the time will come.
5. 65, divided, reminds us of the marrying of the younger sister of king Tî-yî, when the sleeves of her the princess were not equal to those of the still younger sister who accompanied her in an inferior capacity. The case suggests the thought of the moon almost full. There will be good fortune.
6. L6, divided, shows the young lady bearing the basket, but without anything in it, and the gentleman slaughtering the sheep, but without blood flowing from it. There will be no advantage in any way.

火雷 ䷶ 豐 ㊄㊄

豐、亨、王、假之、勿憂、宜日中。

象曰、豐、大也。明以動、故、豐。王假之、尚大也、勿憂宜日中、宜照天下也。日中則昃、月盈則食、天地盈虛、與時消息、而況於人乎 況於鬼神乎

象曰、雷電皆至豐、君子以、折獄致刑。

初九、遇其配主、雖旬、无咎、往、有尚。象曰、雖旬无咎、過旬、災也。

六二、豐其蔀、日中見斗、往、得疑疾、有孚發若、吉。象曰、有孚發若、信以發志也。

九三、豐其沛、日中見沬、折其右肱、无咎。象曰、豐其沛、不可大事也、折其右肱、終不可用也。

九四、豐其蔀、日中見斗、遇其夷主、吉。象曰、豐其蔀、位不當也、日中見斗、幽不明也、遇其夷主、吉行也。

六五、來章、有慶譽、吉。象曰、六五之吉、有慶也。

上六、豐其屋、蔀其家、闚其戶、闃其无人、三歲、不覿、凶。象曰、豐其屋、天際翔也、闚其戶闃其无人、自藏也。

풍豊은 형통하니 왕이라야 이르게 된다. 근심하지 말고 해가 중천에 있는 것이 마땅하다.

초9는 그 짝이 되는 주인을 만나되, 비록 균등하나 허물이 없으니, 가면 숭상함이 있을 것이다.
62는 풍대한 것을 덮어서 가리고 대낮에 북두성을 보니, 가면 의심의 병을 얻을 것이다. 믿음을 두어 마음을 펴면 길할 것이다.
93은 풍대한 것에 장막을 쳤으니 대낮에 작은 별이 보일 것이요, 그 오른팔이 꺾이니 허물이 없다.
94는 풍대한 것을 가리고, 대낮에 북두칠성을 보니, 그 평등한 주인를 만나면 길할 것이다.
65는 와서 빛나면, 경사와 명예가 있어서 길할 것이다.
상6은 그 집을 크게 하고 그 집을 덮은 것이다. 그 문을 엿보니 고요하고 사람이 없어서 삼 년을 보지 못하니 흉하다.

Li intimates progress and development. When a king has reached the point which the name denotes there is no occasion to be anxious through fear of a change. Let him be as the sun at noon.

1. F9, undivided, shows its subject meeting with his mate. Though they are both of the same character, there will be no error. Advance will call forth approval.
2. 62, divided, shows its subject surrounded by screens so large and thick that at midday he can see from them the constellation of the Bushel. If he go and try to enlighten his ruler who is thus emblemed, he will make himself to be viewed with suspicion and dislike. Let him cherish his feeling of sincere devotion that he may thereby move his ruler's mind, and there will be good fortune.
3. 93, undivided, shows its subject with an additional screen of a large and thick banner, through which at midday he can see the small Mei star. In the darkness he breaks his right arm; but there will be no error.
4. 94, undivided, shows its subject in a tent so large and thick that at midday he can see from it the constellation of the Bushel. But he meets with the subject of the first line, undivided like himself. There will be good fortune.
5. 65, divided, shows its subject bringing around him the men of brilliant ability. There will be occasion for congratulation and praise. There will be good fortune.
6. L6, divided, shows its subject with his house made large, but only serving as a screen to his household. When he looks at his door, it is still, and there is nobody about it. For three years no one is to be seen. There will be evil.

山火 旅 ㊄㊅

旅、小亨、旅貞、吉。

象曰、旅小亨、柔得中乎外而順乎剛、止而麗乎明、是以小亨旅貞吉也。旅之時義大矣哉！

象曰、山上有火旅、君子以、明愼用刑、而不留獄。

初六、旅瑣瑣、斯其所取災。象曰、旅瑣瑣、志窮、災也。

六二、旅卽次、懷其資、得童僕貞。象曰、得童僕貞、終无尤也。

九三、旅焚其次、喪其童僕貞厲。象曰、旅焚其次、亦以傷矣、以旅與下、其義喪也。

九四、旅于處、得其資斧、我心、不快。象曰、旅于處、未得位也、得其資斧、心未快也。

六五、射雉一失亡、終以譽命。象曰、終以譽命、上逮也。

上九、鳥焚其巢、旅人、先笑後號咷、喪牛于易、凶。象曰、以旅在上、其義焚也、喪牛于易、終莫之聞也。

여旅는 조금 형통하고 나그네가 바르게 해서 길하다.

초6은 나그네가 자질구레하니, 이는 재앙을 취하는 바이다.
62는 나그네가 여관에 들어가고, 노자를 가지며, 어린 종의 바름을 갖춘다.
93은 나그네가 그 여관을 불사르고, 어린 종의 바름을 잃으니 위태롭다.
94는 나그네가 쉴 자리에서 노자와 도끼를 얻었으니, 내 마음이 유쾌하지 않다.
65는 꿩을 화살 한 대로 쏘았으나 없어져 버렸으니, 마침내 명예로운 명을 받게 될 것이다.
상9는 새가 그 집을 태우니, 나그네가 먼저는 웃고 뒤에는 울부짖는다. 소를 쉽게 잃으니 흉하다.

Lu intimates that in the condition which it denotes there may be some little attainment and progress. If the stranger or traveller be firm and correct as he ought to be, there will be good fortune.

1. F6, divided, shows the stranger mean and meanly occupied. It is thus that he brings on himself further calamity.
2. 62, divided, shows the stranger, occupying his lodging-house, carrying with him his means of livelihood, and provided with good and trusty servants.
3. 93, undivided, shows the stranger, burning his lodging-house, and having lost his servants. However firm and correct he try to be, he will be in peril.
4. 94, undivided, shows the traveller in a resting-place, having also the means of livelihood and the axe, but still saying, 'I am not at ease in my mind.'
5. 65, divided, shows its subject shooting a pheasant. He will lose his arrow, but in the end he will obtain praise and a high charge.
6. L9, undivided, suggests the idea of a bird burning its nest. The stranger, thus represented, first laughs and then cries out. He has lost his ox-like docility too readily and easily. There will be evil.

風重 ䷸ 巽 ㊼

巽、小亨、利有攸往、利見大人。

象曰、重巽、以申命。剛、巽乎中正而志行、柔皆順乎剛、是以小亨、利有攸往、利見大人。

象曰、隨風、巽、君子以、中命行事。

初六、進退、利武人之貞。象曰、進退、志疑也、利武人之貞、志治也。

九二、巽在牀下、用史巫紛若、吉、无咎。象曰、紛若之吉、得中也。

九三、頻巽、吝。象曰、頻巽之吝、志窮也。

六四、悔亡、田獲三品。象曰、田獲三品、有功也。

九五、貞、吉、悔亡、无不利、无初有終、先庚三日、後庚三日、吉。象曰、九五之吉、位正中也。

上九、巽在牀下、喪其資斧、貞、凶。象曰、巽在牀下、上窮也、喪其資斧、正乎、凶也。

손巽은 조금 형통하니 가는 바가 있음이 이로우며, 대인을 만나봄이 이롭다.

초6은 나가갔다가 물러가니, 무인武人의 바름이 이롭다.
92는 겸손하여 평상 아래에 있으니, 사무史巫를 쓰면 성대하게 길하고 허물이 없을 것이다.
93은 찡그리며 겸손한 것이니, 궁색할 것이다.
64는 후회가 없어지니, 사냥하여 삼품三品을 얻는다.
95는 바르면 길해서 후회가 없으며 이롭지 않음이 없으니, 처음은 없지만 마침은 있다. 사흘 전에 미리 명령을 펴며, 다시 사흘 후에 명령을 펴면 길할 것이다.
상9는 상 아래에서 너무 겸손하여 쓰는 도끼를 잃으니, 바름이 흉할 것이다.

Xun intimates that under the conditions which it denotes there will be some little attainment and progress. There will be advantage in movement onward in whatever direction. It will be advantageous also to see the great man.

1. F6, divided, shows its subject now advancing, now receding. It would be advantageous for him to have the firm correctness of a brave soldier.
2. 92, undivided, shows the representative of Sun beneath a couch, and employing diviners and exorcists in a way bordering on confusion. There will be good fortune and no error.
3. 93, undivided, shows its subject penetrating only by violent and repeated efforts. There will be occasion for regret.
4. 64, divided, shows all occasion for repentance in its subject passed away. He takes game for its threefold use in his hunting.
5. 95, undivided, shows that with firm correctness there will be good fortune to its subject. All occasion for repentance will disappear, and all his movements will be advantageous. There may have been no good beginning, but there will be a good end. Three days before making any changes, let him give notice of them; and three days after, let him reconsider them. There will thus be good fortune.
6. L9, undivided, shows the representative of penetration beneath a couch, and having lost the axe with which he executed his decisions. However firm and correct he may try to be, there will be evil.

澤重 ䷹ 兌 五八

兌、亨、利貞。

象曰、兌、說也。剛中而柔外、說以利貞。是以順乎天而應乎人。說以先民、民忘其勞、說以犯難、民忘其死、說之大民勸矣哉！

象曰、麗澤、兌、君子以、朋友講習。

初九、和兌、吉。象曰、和兌之吉、行未疑也。

九二、孚兌、吉、悔亡。象曰、孚兌之吉、信志也。

六三、來兌、凶。象曰、來兌之凶、位不當也。

九四、商兌未寧、介疾、有喜。象曰、九四之喜、有慶也。

九五、孚于剝、有厲。象曰、孚于剝、位正當也！

上六、引兌。象曰、上六引兌、未光也。

태兌는 형통하니 바르게 함이 이롭다.

초9는 화합해서 기뻐하니, 길하다.
92는 미덥고 기뻐하나, 길해야 후회가 없을 것이다.
63은 와서 기뻐함이니, 흉하다.
94는 헤아려 기뻐하되 편안하지 아니하여 병통을 막으니, 기쁨이 있을 것이다.
95는 깎는데 믿으면 위태함이 있을 것이다.
상6은 이끌려서 기뻐함이다.

Dui intimates that under its conditions there will be progress and attainment. But it will be advantageous to be firm and correct.

1. F9, undivided, shows the pleasure of inward harmony. There will be good fortune.
2. 92, undivided, shows the pleasure arising from inward sincerity. There will be good fortune. Occasion for repentance will disappear.
3. 63, divided, shows its subject bringing round himself whatever can give pleasure. There will be evil.
4. 94, undivided, shows its subject deliberating about what to seek his pleasure in, and not at rest. He borders on what would be injurious, but there will be cause for joy.
5. 95, undivided, shows its subject trusting in one who would injure him. The situation is perilous.
6. L6, divided, shows the pleasure of its subject in leading and attracting others.

水風 ䷺ 渙 (五九)

渙、亨、王假有廟、利涉大川、利貞。

象曰、渙亨、剛、來而不窮、柔得位乎外而上同。王假有廟、王乃在中也、利涉大川、乘木、有功也。

象曰、風行水上、渙、先王以、享于帝、立廟。

初六、用拯、馬壯、吉。象曰、初六之吉、順也。

九二、渙、奔其机、悔亡。象曰、渙奔其机、得願也。

六三、渙、其躬、无悔。象曰、渙其躬、志在外也。

六四、渙、其羣、元吉、渙、有丘、匪夷所思。象曰、渙其羣元吉、光大也。

九五、渙、汗其大號、渙、王居、无咎。象曰、王居无咎、正位也。

上九、渙、其血、去、逖出、无咎。象曰、渙其血、遠害也。

환渙은 형통하니 왕이 사당에 이르며, 큰 내를 건너는 것이 이롭고 바르게 함이 이롭다.

초6은 구원하되 말이 장대하니 길하다.
92는 흩어짐에 그 평상에 달려가면, 후회가 없을 것이다.
63은 흩어짐에 그 몸이 후회가 없을 것이다.
64는 흩어짐에 그 무리로써 함이다. 크게 길하니 흩어짐에 언덕처럼 평온하지 못한 생각이 있다.
95는 흩어짐에 땀을 흘리며 크게 부르짖으니, 흩어짐에 왕이 거주해야 허물이 없을 것이다.
상9는 그 피를 흩어버리고 가되, 멀리 나가면 허물이 없을 것이다.

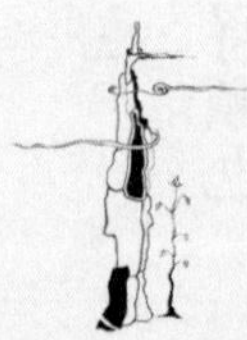

Huan intimates that under its conditions there will be progress and success. The king goes to his ancestral temple ; and it will be advantageous to cross the great stream. It will be advantageous to be firm and correct.

1. F6, divided, shows its subject engaged in rescuing from the impending evil and having the assistance of a strong horse. There will be good fortune.
2. 92, undivided, shows its subject, amid the dispersion, hurrying to his contrivance for security. All occasion for repentance will disappear.
3. 63, divided, shows its subject discarding any regard to his own person. There will be no occasion for repentance.
4. 64, divided, shows its subject scattering the different parties in the state; which leads to great good fortune. From the dispersion he collects again good men standing out, a crowd like a mound, which is what ordinary men would not have thought of.
5. 95, undivided, shows its subject amidst the dispersion issuing his great announcements as the perspiration flows from his body. He scatters abroad also the accumulations in the royal granaries. There will be no error.
6. L9, undivided, shows its subject disposing of what may be called its bloody wounds, and going and separating himself from its anxious fears. There will be no error.

澤水 ䷻ 節 (六十)

節、亨、苦節、不可貞。

彖曰、節亨、剛柔分而剛得中。苦節不可貞、其道窮也。說以行險、當位以節、中正以通。天地節而四時成、節以制度、不傷財、不害民。

象曰、澤上有水、節、君子以、制數度、議德行。

初六、不出戶庭、无咎。象曰、不出戶庭、知通塞也。

九二、不出門庭、凶。象曰、不出門庭凶、失時極也。

六三、不節若、則嗟若、无咎。象曰、不節之嗟、又誰咎也！

六四、安節、亨。象曰、安節之亨、承上道也。

九五、甘節、吉、往、有尚。象曰、甘節之吉、居位中也。

上六、苦節、貞、凶、悔、亡。象曰、苦節貞凶、其道窮也。

절節은 형통하니 고통스러운 절제는 바르게 할 수 없을 것이다.

초9는 방문 밖의 뜰에 나서지 않으면 허물이 없을 것이다.
92는 문밖 뜰에 나서지 않는 것이니, 흉하다.
63은 절제하지 않아서 탄식할 것이니, 허물이 없다.
64는 편안하게 절제하니, 형통할 것이다.
95는 달갑게 절제하여 길하니, 가면 가상함이 있을 것이다.
상6은 고통스럽게 절제함이니, 바르게 하면 흉은 되나 후회는 없을 것이다.

Jie intimates that under its conditions there will be progress and attainment. But if the regulations which it prescribes be severe and difficult, they cannot be permanent.

1. F9, undivided, shows its subject not quitting the courtyard outside his door. There will be no error.
2. 92, undivided, shows its subject not quitting the courtyard inside his gate. There will be evil.
3. 63, divided, shows its subject with no appearance of observing the proper regulations, in which case we shall see him lamenting. But three will be no one to blame but himself.
4. 64, divided, shows its subject quietly and naturally attentive to all regulations. There will be progress and success.
5. 95, undivided, shows its subject sweetly and acceptably enacting his regulations. There will be good fortune. The onward progress with them will afford ground for admiration.
6. L6, divided, shows its subject enacting regulations severe and difficult. Even with firmness and correctness there will be evil. But though there will be cause for repentance, it will by and by disappear.

風澤 中孚 (六一)

中孚、豚魚、吉、利涉大川、利貞。

彖曰、中孚、柔在內而剛得中、說而巽、孚乃化邦也。豚魚吉、信及豚魚也、利涉大川、乘木、舟虛也、中孚、以利貞、乃應乎天也。

象曰、澤上有風、中孚、君子以、議獄、緩死。

初九、虞、吉、有他、不燕。象曰、初九虞吉、志未變也。

九二、鳴鶴、在陰、其子和之、我有好爵、吾與爾靡之。象曰、其子和之、中心願也。

六三、得敵、或鼓或罷或泣或歌。象曰、或鼓或罷、位不當也。

六四、月幾望、馬匹、亡、无咎。象曰、馬匹亡、絶類、上也。

九五、有孚攣如、无咎。象曰、有孚攣如、位正當也。

上九、翰音、登于天、貞、凶。象曰、翰音登于天、何可長也!

중부中孚는 돼지와 물고기에까지 믿음이 미치면 길하니, 큰 내를 건넘이 이롭고 바르게 함이 이롭다.

초9는 전일해서 길하니, 다른 것이 있으면 편안하지 못할 것이다.
92는 우는 학鶴이 그늘에 있어서 그 새끼가 화답한다. 나에게 좋은 술잔이 있어서 나와 너가 함께 나눈다.
63은 적을 만나서 북을 치거나 그치며, 울거나 노래한다.
64는 달이 거의 보름이니, 말의 짝이 없어지면 허물이 없을 것이다.
95는 믿음에 매여야 허물이 없을 것이다.
상9는 높이 나는 소리가 하늘에 오르니, 바르게 하더라도 흉하다.

Zhongfu moves even pigs and fish, and leads to good fortune. There will be advantage in crossing the great stream. There will be advantage in being firm and correct.

1. F9, undivided, shows its subject resting in himself. there will be good fortune. If he sought to any other, he would not find rest.

2. 92, undivided, shows its subject like the crane crying out in her hidden retirement, and her young ones responding to her. It is as if it were said, 'I have a cup of good spirits,' and the response were, 'I will partake of it with you.'

3. 63, divided, shows its subject having met with his mate. Now he beats his drum, and now he leaves off. Now he weeps, and now he sings.

4. 64, divided, shows its subject like the moon nearly full, and like a horse in a chariot whose fellow disappears. There will be no error.

5. 95, undivided, shows its subject perfectly sincere, and linking others to him in closest union. There will be no error.

6. L9, undivided, shows subject in chanticleer trying to mount to heaven. Even with firm correctness there will be evil.

山雷 ䷽ 小過 ㊷

小過、亨、利貞、可小事、不可大事、飛鳥遺之音、不宜上、宜下、大吉。

彖曰、小過、小者過而亨也、過以利貞、與時行也。柔得中、是以小事吉也、剛失位而不中、是以不可大事也。有飛鳥之象焉、飛鳥遺之音不宜上宜下大吉、上逆而下順也。

象曰、山上有雷小過、君子以、行過乎恭、喪過乎哀、用過乎儉。

初六、飛鳥、以凶。象曰、飛鳥以凶、不可如何也。

六二、過其祖、遇其妣、不及其君、遇其臣、无咎。象曰、不及其君、臣不可過也。

九三、弗過防之、從或戕之、凶。象曰、從或戕之、凶如何也！

九四、无咎、弗過、遇之、往、厲、必戒、勿用永貞。象曰、弗過遇之、位不當也、往厲必戒、終不可長也。

六五、密雲不雨、自我西郊、公、弋取彼在穴。象曰、密雲不雨、已上也。

上六、弗遇、過之、飛鳥離之、凶、是謂災眚。象曰、弗遇過之、已亢也。

소과小過는 형통하니 곧음이 이롭다. 작은 일은 가하고 큰 일은 가하지 않으니, 나는 새가 소리를 남김에 올라가서는 안 되고 내려온다면 크게 길할 것이다.

초6은 나는 새니, 흉할 것이다.
62는 그 할아버지를 지나서 그 할머니를 만나니 그 임금에까지 미치지 않는다. 그 신하를 만나면 허물이 없을 것이다.
93은 지나쳐서 막지 못하고 좇으니, 혹 해치는지라 흉할 것이다.
94는 허물이 없어서 지나치지 아니하여 만나니, 가면 위태롭다. 반드시 경계해야 하며, 길이 바르게 하는 데에 쓰지 않아야 할 것이다.
65는 구름이 짙어도 비가 오지 않음은 내가 서교西郊로부터 하는 것이니, 공公이 구멍 속에 숨어 있는 것을 쏘아 잡는다.
상6은 만나지 않고 지나치니, 나는 새가 떠나는 것이다. 흉하니 이를 일러 재앙이라고 한다.

Xiaoguo indicates that in the circumstances which it implies there will be progress and attainment. But it will be advantageous to be firm and correct. What the name denotes may be done in small affairs, but not in great affairs. It is like the notes that come down from a bird on the wing;-to descend is better than to ascend. There will in this way be great good fortune.

1. F6, divided, suggests the idea of a bird flying, and ascending till the issue is evil.
2. 62, divided, shows its subject passing by his grandfather, and meeting with his grandmother; not attempting anything against his ruler, but meeting him as his minister. There will be no error.
3. 93, undivided, shows its subject taking no extraordinary precautions against danger; and some in consequence finding opportunity to assail and injure him. There will be evil.
4. 94, undivided, shows its subject falling into no error, but meeting the exigency of his situation, without exceeding in his natural course. If he go forward, there will be peril, and he must be cautious. There is no occasion to be using firmness perpetually.
5. 65, divided, suggests the idea of dense clouds, but no rain, coming from our borders in the west. It also shows the prince shooting his arrow, and taking the bird in a cave.
6. L6, divided, shows its subject not meeting the exigency of his situation, and exceeding his proper course. It suggests the idea of a bird flying far aloft. There will be evil. The case is what is called one of calamity and self-produced injury.

水火 既濟 ䷾ (六三)

既濟、亨、小、利貞、初吉、終亂。

彖曰、既濟亨、小者亨也。利貞、剛柔正而位當也。初吉、柔得中也、終止則亂、其道窮也。

象曰、水在火上、既濟、君子以、思患而豫防之。

初九、曳其輪、濡其尾、无咎。象曰、曳其輪、義无咎也。

六二、婦喪其茀、勿逐、七日、得。象曰、七日得、以中道也。

九三、高宗、伐鬼方、三年克之、小人勿用。象曰、三年克之、憊也。

六四、繻、有衣袽、終日戒。象曰、終日戒、有所疑也。

九五、東鄰殺牛、不如西鄰之禴祭、實受其福。象曰、東鄰殺牛、不如西鄰之時也、實受其福、吉大來也。

上六、濡其首、厲。象曰、濡其首厲、何可久也！

기제既濟는 작은 것도 형통하게 하여 곧음이 이로우니, 처음은 길하고 마침은 어지럽다.

초9는 그 바퀴를 끌고 그 꼬리를 적시니, 허물이 없을 것이다.

62는 지어미가 머리장식을 잃으니, 쫓지 않아도 칠일만에 얻을 것이다.

93은 고종高宗이 귀방鬼方을 쳐서 삼년 만에 이기니 소인을 쓰지 말 것이다.

64는 배가 새니, 옷가지를 준비해두고 종일토록 경계해야 할 것이다.

95는 동쪽 이웃의 소를 죽이는 것이, 서쪽 이웃의 간략한 제사로써 그 복을 받는 것보다 못하다.

상6은 그 머리를 적시니, 위태롭다.

Jigi intimates progress and success in small matters. There will be advantage in being firm and correct. There has been good fortune in the beginning ; there may be disorder in the end.

1. F9, undivided, shows its subject as a driver who drags back his wheel, or as a fox which has wet his tail. There will be no error.

2. 62, divided, shows its subject as a wife who has lost her carriage-screen. There is no occasion to go in pursuit of it. In seven days she will find it.

3. 93, undivided, suggests the case of Kâo 3ung who attacked the Demon region, but was three years in subduing it. Small men should not be employed in such enterprises.

4. 64, divided, shows its subject with rags provided against any leak in his boat, and on his guard all day long.

5. 95, undivided, shows its subject as the neighbour in the east who slaughters an ox for his sacrifice ; but this is not equal to the small spring sacrifice of the neighbour in the west, whose sincerity receives the blessing.

6. L6, divided, shows its subject with even his head immersed. The position is perilous.

水火 ䷿ 未濟 ㊅㊃

未濟、亨、小狐汔濟、濡其尾、无攸利。

象曰、未濟亨、柔得中也。小狐汔濟、未出中也、濡其尾无攸利、不續終也。雖不當位、剛柔應也。

象曰、火在水上、未濟、君子以、愼辨物、居方。

初六、濡其尾、吝。象曰、濡其尾、亦不知極也。

九二、曳其輪、貞、吉。象曰、九二貞吉、中以行正也。

六三、未濟、征、凶、利涉大川。象曰、未濟征凶、位不當也。

九四、貞、吉、悔亡、震用伐鬼方、三年、有賞于大國。象曰、貞吉悔亡、志行也。

六五、貞、吉、无悔、君子之光、有孚、吉。象曰、君子之光、其暉吉也。

上九、有孚于飮酒、无咎、濡其首、有孚、失是。象曰、飮酒濡首、亦不知節也。

미제未濟는 형통하니, 어린 여우가 거의 물이 없는 데로 건너다가 그 꼬리를 적시니, 이로울 것이 없다.

초6은 그 꼬리를 적시니, 궁색하다.

92는 그 바퀴를 당기면, 바르게 해서 길할 것이다.

63은 건너지 못하여 가면 흉하지만, 큰 내를 건너는 것이 이로울 것이다.

94는 바르게 하면 길해서 후회가 없을 것이니, 위엄을 떨쳐 귀방鬼方을 쳐서 삼년에야 큰 나라로 상을 받는다.

65는 바르면 길하여 후회가 없으니, 군자의 빛남이다. 믿어주면 길할 것이다.

상9는 믿음을 두어 술을 마시면 허물이 없지만, 그 머리를 적시면 믿는데서 잃을 것이다.

Weiji intimates progress and success in the circumstances which it implies. We see a young fox that has nearly crossed the stream, when its tail gets immersed. There will be no advantage in any way.

1. F6, divided, shows its subject like a fox whose tail gets immersed. There will be occasion for regret.

2. 92, undivided, shows its subject dragging back his carriage-wheel. With firmness and correctness there will be good fortune.

3. 63, divided, shows its subject, with the state of things not yet remedied, advancing on ; which will lead to evil. But there will be advantage in trying to cross the great stream.

4. 94, undivided, shows its subject by firm correctness obtaining good fortune, so that all occasion for repentance disappears. Let him stir himself up, as if he were invading the Demon region, where for three years rewards will come to him and his troops from the great kingdom.

5. 65, divided, shows its subject by firm correctness obtaining good fortune, and having no occasion for repentance. We see in him the brightness of a superior man, and the possession of sincerity. There will be good fortune.

6. L9, undivided, shows its subject full of confidence and therefore feasting quietly. There will be no error. If he cherish this confidence, till he is like the fox who gets his head immersed, it will fail of what is right.

●天尊地卑、乾坤、定矣。卑高以陳、貴賤、位矣。動靜有常、剛柔斷矣。方以類聚、物以羣分、吉凶、生矣。在天成象、在地成形、變化、見矣。

●是故、剛柔相摩、八卦相盪、○鼓之以雷霆、潤之以風雨、日月、運行、一寒一暑。○乾道成男、坤道成女。○乾知大始、坤作成物。

●乾以易知、坤以簡能、○易則易知、簡則易從、易知則有親、易從則有功、有親則可久、有功則可大、可久則賢人之德、可大則賢人之業。○易簡而天下之理得矣、天下之理得而成位乎其中矣。（以上 第一章）

●聖人、設卦、觀象繫辭焉、而明吉凶、○剛柔相推、而生變化。○是故、吉凶者、失得之象也、悔吝者、憂虞之象也。○變化者、進退之象也、剛柔者、晝夜之象也、六爻之動、三極之道也。

●是故、君子所居而安者、易之序也、所樂而玩者、爻之辭也。○是故、君子居則觀其象而玩其辭、動則觀其變而玩其占、是以自天祐之、吉无不利。

（以上 第二章）

하늘은 높고 땅은 낮으니 건乾과 곤坤이 정해지고, 높고 낮은 것이 베풀어지니 귀함과 천함이 자리를 잡는다. 움직이고 고요함에 항상恒常함이 있으니 강건한 것과 부드러운 것이 판단되고, 종류가 유사한 것끼리 모이고, 사물은 무리끼리 나뉘니, 길흉이 생겨난다. 하늘에서는 형상을 이루고, 땅에서는 형태를 이루니, 변화가 나타난다.

Heaven is lofty and honourable; earth is low. Their symbols, *Qian* and *Kun*, with their respective meanings, were determined in accordance with this. Things low and high appear displayed in a similar relation. The upper and lower trigrams, and the relative position of individual lines, as noble and mean, had their places assigned accordingly. Movement and rest are the regular qualities of their respective subjects. Hence comes the definite distinction of the several lines as the strong and the weak. Affairs are arranged together according to their tendencies, and things are divided according to their classes. Hence were produced the interpretations in the *Yi*, concerning what is good or lucky and evil or unlucky. In the heavens there are the different figures there completed, and on the earth there are the different bodies there formed. Corresponding to them were the changes and transformations exhibited in the *Yi*.

이런 고로 강건한 것과 부드러운 것이 서로 갈마들고 팔괘八卦가 서로 움직여 번개와 우뢰로써 고동鼓動시키며, 바람과 비로써 적셔주고, 해와 달이 운행하여 한번 추우면 한번 더워진다. 건도乾道는 남자를 이루고 곤도坤道는 여자를 이루니 건乾은 큰 시작을 알고 곤坤은 만물을 만든다.
건乾은 쉽게 알고 곤坤은 간단함으로 능하니, 쉬우면 알기 쉽고 간단하면 따르기 쉽다. 알기 쉬우면 친근함이 있고, 따르기 쉬우면 공功이 있으며,

After this fashion a strong and a weak line were manipulated together till there were the eight trigrams, and those eight trigrams were added, each to itself and to all the others, till the sixty-four hexagrams were formed. We have the exciting forces of thunder and lightning; the fertilising influences of wind and rain; and the revolutions of the sun and moon, which give rise to cold and warmth. The attributes expressed by *Qian* constitute the male; those expressed by *Kun* constitute the female. *Qian* symbolises Heaven, which directs the great beginnings of things; *Kun* symbolises Earth, which gives to them their completion.
It is by the ease with which it proceeds that *Qian* directs as it does, and by its unhesitating response that *Kun* exhibits such ability. He who attains to this ease of Heaven will be easily understood, and he who attains to this freedom from laborious effort of the Earth will be easily followed. He who is easily understood will have adherents, and he who is easily followed will achieve success.

친근하면 오래 갈 수 있고, 공功이 있으면 커질 수 있다. 오래 갈 수 있으면 현인의 덕이요, 클 수 있으면 현인의 업業이다. 쉽고 간단해서 천하의 이치를 얻으니, 천하의 이치를 얻으면 가운데에서 자리를 이룬다.
성인은 괘를 설치하고 상象을 관찰하며, 말을 붙여서 길흉을 밝히며, 강剛과 유柔가 서로를 미루어서 변화를 생성시킨다. 이런 까닭에 길흉이란 것은 잃고 얻는 상象이요, 후회와 궁색함이란 근심하고 걱정하는 상象이다.

He who has adherents can continue long, and he who achieves success can become great. To be able to continue long shows the virtue of the wise and able man; to be able to become great is the heritage he will acquire. With the attainment of such ease and such freedom from laborious effort, the mastery is got of all principles under the sky. With the attainment of that mastery, the sage makes good his position in the middle between heaven and earth.
The sages set forth the diagrams, inspected the emblems contained in them, and appended their explanations;—in this way the good fortune and bad indicated by them were made clear. The strong and the weak lines displace each other, and produce the changes and transformations in the figures. Therefore the good fortune and evil mentioned in the explanations are the indications of the right and wrong in men's conduct of affairs, and the repentance and regret similarly mentioned are the indications of their sorrow and anxiety.

변화란 나아가고 물러가는 상象이요, 강유剛柔란 것은 낮과 밤의 상象이요, 육효六爻의 움직임은 삼극三極의 도道이다.
이런 까닭에 군자가 편안하게 거처하는 바는 역易의 차례요, 즐기면서 노는 것은 효爻의 말이다. 이런 까닭에 군자는 거처할 때는 그 상을 관찰하여 그 말의 뜻을 새겨보고, 움직일 때는 그 변화를 관찰해서 그 점의 의미를 완미한다. 이렇게 함으로써 하늘로부터 도움을 받으니 길하여 이롭지 않음이 없다.

The changes and transformations of the lines are the emblems of the advance and retrogression of the vital force in nature. Thus what we call the strong and the weak lines become the emblems of day and night. The movements which take place in the six places of the hexagram show the course of the three extremes i. e. of the three Powers in their perfect operation.
Therefore what the superior man rests in, in whatever position he is placed, is the order shown in the *Yi*; and the study which gives him the greatest pleasure is that of the explanations of the several lines. Therefore the superior man, when living quietly, contemplates the emblems and studies the explanations of them; when initiating any movement, he contemplates the changes that are made in divining, and studies the prognostications from them. Thus 'is help extended to him from Heaven; there will be good fortune, and advantage in every movement.'

단彖은 상象을 말한 것이요, 효爻는 변화를 말한 것이다. 길흉은 그 득실을 말한 것이요, 회린悔吝은 그 작은 흠을 말하는 것이요, 허물이 없다는 것은 허물을 잘 고친 것이다. 이런 까닭에 귀천은 그 자리에 달려 있고, 작고 큰 것을 변별하는 것은 괘사에 있으며, 길흉을 분별하는 것은 효사에 있고, 회린을 근심하는 것은 분별함에 있으며, 움직여서 허물이 없도록 하는 것은 후회함에 있다.

The *Tuan* speak of the emblematic figures of the complete diagrams. The *Yao* speak of the changes taking place in the several lines. The expressions about good fortune or bad are used with reference to the figures and lines, as being right or wrong according to theA conditions of time and place; those about repentance or regret refer to small faults in the satisf ying those conditions; when it is said 'there will be no error,' or 'no blame,' there is reference to the subject repairing an error by what is good. Therefore the distinction of the upper and lower trigrams and of the individual lines as noble or mean is decided by the relative position of the lines; the regulations of small and great are found in the diagrams, and the discriminations of good and bad fortune appear in the subjoined explanations. Anxiety against having occasion for repentance or regret should be felt at the boundary line between good and evil. The stirring up the thought of securing that there shall be no blame arises from the feeling of repentance.

●彖者、言乎象者也、爻者、言乎變者也。○吉凶者、言乎其失得也、悔吝者、言乎其小疵也、无咎者、善補過也。○是故、列貴賤者、存乎位、齊小大者、存乎卦、辨吉凶者、存乎辭、○憂悔吝者、存乎介、震无咎者、存乎悔。○是故、卦有小大、辭有險易、辭也者、各指其所之。(以上 第三章)

●易、與天地準、故、能彌綸天地之道。○仰以觀於天文、俯以察於地理、是故、知幽明之故、原始反終、故、知死生之說、精氣爲物、遊魂爲變、是故、知鬼神之情狀。○與天地相似、故、不違、知周乎萬物而道濟天下、故、不過、旁行而不流、樂天知命、故、不憂、安土、敦乎仁、故、能愛。

●範圍天地之化而不過、曲成萬物而不遺、通乎晝夜之道而知、故、神无方而易无體。(以上 第四章)

●一陰一陽之謂道。○繼之者善也、成之者性也。○仁者見之、謂之仁、知者見之、謂之知、百姓、日用而不知、故、君子之道鮮矣。○顯諸仁、藏諸用、鼓萬物而不與聖人同憂、盛德大業、至矣哉。○富有之謂大業、日新之謂盛德。

이런 까닭에 괘에는 작고 큰 것이 있으며, 말에는 험한 것과 쉬운 것이 있으니, 말이라는 것은 각기 그 가는 바를 가리키는 것이다.
역易이 천지와 더불어 들어맞는다. 그러므로 능히 천지의 도道를 합쳐서 다스릴 수 있다. 우러러서 천문天文을 보고 굽혀서 지리地理를 살핀다. 이런 까닭에 보이지 않는 세계와 보이는 세계의 연고를 알며, 처음을 근원으로 하여 나중으로 돌아온다. 그러므로 죽고 사는 말을 알며, 깨끗한 기운이 사물이 되고 혼魂이 노는 것이 변하게 된다. 이런 까닭에 귀신의 실상을 알게 된다.

Thus of the diagrams some are small, and some are great; and of the explanations some are startling, and some are unexciting. Every one of those explanations has reference to the tendencies indicated by the symbols.
The *Yi* was made on a principle of accordance with heaven and earth, and shows us therefore, without rent or confusion, the course of things in heaven and earth. The sage, in accordance with the *Yi*, looking up, contemplates the brilliant phenomena of the heavens, and, looking down, examines the definite arrangements of the earth;—thus he knows the causes of darkness or, what is obscure and light or, what is bright. He traces things to their beginning, and follows them to their end;—thus he knows what can be said about death and life. He perceives how the union of essence and breath form things, and the disappearance or wandering away of the soul produces the change of their constitution;—thus he knows the characteristics of the anima and animus.

천지와 더불어 같으므로 어긋나지 않으니, 앎은 만물에 두루 미치고, 도道는 천하를 구제하므로 잘못되지 않고, 두루 행해도 흘러넘치지 않으며, 하늘을 즐거워하고 천명을 안다. 그러므로 근심치 않으며, 흙에 편안해서 아주 인자하다. 그러므로 능히 사랑한다.
천지의 변화를 본떠서 지나치지 않고, 만물을 곡진히 이루어서 빠뜨리지 않으며, 낮과 밤의 도에 통하여 안다. 그러므로 신은 방소方所가 없고 역易은 몸체가 없다.

There is a similarity between him and heaven and earth, and hence there is no contrariety in him to them. His knowledge embraces all things, and his course is intended to be helpful to all under the sky;—and hence he falls into no error. He acts according to the exigency of circumstances without being carried away by their current; he rejoices in Heaven and knows its ordinations;—and hence he has no anxieties. He rests in his own present position, and cherishes; the spirit of generous benevolence;—and hence he can love without reserve.
Through the *Yi*, he comprehends as in a mould or enclosure the transformations of heaven and earth without any error; by an ever-varying adaptation he completes the nature of all things without exception; he penetrates to a knowledge of the course of day and night and all other connected phenomena;—it is thus that his operation is spirit-like, unconditioned by place, while the changes which he produces are not restricted to any form.

한번 음陰하고 한번 양陽하는 것을 일러서 도道라고 하니, 이를 계승하는 것은 선善이요, 이를 이룬 것은 성性이다. 어진 자는 이것을 보고 인仁이라 말하며, 지혜있는 자는 이것을 보고 지知라 말하며, 백성은 매일 쓰면서도 알지 못한다. 그러므로 군자의 도道가 드물다. 인仁을 드러내고 용用을 감추어 만물을 고동鼓動시키되 성인과 더불어 함께 근심치 않으니, 성대한 덕업이 지극하다. 풍부하게 갖고 있는 것을 위대한 사업이라고 말하며, 날마다 새로워지는 것을 성대한 덕이라 말한다.

The successive movement of the inactive and active operations constitutes what is called the course of things. That which ensues as the result of their movement is goodness; that which shows it in its completeness is the natures of men and things. The benevolent see it and call it benevolence. The wise see it and call it wisdom. The common people, acting daily according to it, yet have no knowledge of it. Thus it is that the course of things, as seen by the superior man, is seen by few. It is manifested in the benevolence of its operations, and then again it conceals and stores up its resources. It gives their stimulus to all things, without having the same anxieties that possess the sage. Complete is its abundant virtue and the greatness of its stores! Its rich possessions is what is intended by 'the greatness of its stores;' the daily renovation which it produces is what is meant by 'the abundance of its virtue.

●生生之謂易、○成象之謂乾、效法之謂坤、○極數知來之謂占、通變之謂事、○陰陽不測之謂神。（以上 第五章）

●夫易、廣矣大矣！以言乎遠則不禦、以言乎邇則靜而正、以言乎天地之間則備矣。○夫乾、其靜也專、其動也直、是以大生焉、夫坤、其靜也翕、其動也闢、是以廣生焉。○廣大、配天地、變通、配四時、陰陽之義、配日月、易簡之善、配至德。（以上 第六章）

●子曰、易、其至矣乎 夫易、聖人、所以崇德而廣業也。知、崇、禮、卑、崇、效天、卑、法地。○天地設位、而易行乎其中矣。成性存存、道義之門。（以上 第七章）

●聖人、有以見天下之賾、而擬諸其形容、象其物宜、是故謂之象。○聖人、有以見天下之動、而觀其會通、以行其典禮、繫辭焉、以斷其吉凶、是故、謂之爻。○言天下之至賾、而不可惡也、言天下之至動、而不可亂也。○擬之而後、言、議之而後、動、擬議、以成其變化。

생성시키고 또 생성시키는 것을 일러서 역易이라 하고, 상象을 이루는 것을 일러서 건乾이라 하며, 법法을 본받는 것을 일러서 곤坤이라 하고, 수數를 끝까지 미루어서 미래를 아는 것을 점占이라 하며, 변하여 통하게 하는 것을 일러서 일이라 하고, 음양陰陽을 측량할 수 없는 것을 신神이라 한다.
대저 역易은 넓고도 크다. 먼 곳에서도 멈추지 않고, 가까운 곳에서는 고요하여 바르게 되며, 천지天地의 사이에서 갖추어져 있다.

Production and reproduction is what is called the process of change. The formation of the semblances shadowy forms of things is what we attribute to *Khien*; the giving to them their specific forms is what we attribute to *Khwan*. The exhaustive use of the numbers that turn up in manipulating the stalks, and thereby knowing the character of coming events, is what we call prognosticating; the comprehension of the changes indicated leads us to what we call the business to be done.
That which is unfathomable in the movement of the inactive and active operations is the presence of a spiritual power.
Yes, *Yi* is wide and great! If we speak of it in its farthest reaching, no limit can be set to it; if we speak of it with reference to what is near at hand, its lessons are still and correct; if we speak of it in connexion with all between heaven and earth, it embraces all.

대저 건乾이란 고요히 있을 때에는 전일하고 움직일 때에는 곧다. 이로써 큰 것이 나온다. 대저 곤坤이란 고요히 있을 때에는 닫히고 움직일 때에는 열린다. 이로써 넓은 것이 나온다. 넓고 큰 것은 천지天地와 부합하고, 변하여 통하는 것은 사계절과 부합하며, 음양陰陽의 뜻은 해와 달과 부합하고, 쉽고 간단한 선善에 지극한 덕과 부합한다.
공자孔子가 말씀하시길, 역易이 그 지극하도다! 대저 역易은 성인이 그로써 덕을 숭상하고 업을 넓히니,

There is *Qian*. In its individual stillness it is self-absorbed; when exerting its motive power it goes straight forward; and thus it is that its productive action is on a grand scale. There is *Khwan*. In its individual stillness, it is self-collected and capacious; when exerting its motive power, it developes its resources, and thus its productive action is on a wide scale. In its breadth and greatness, the *Yi* corresponds to heaven and earth; in its ever-recurring changes, it corresponds to the four seasons; in its mention of the bright or active, and the dark or inactive operation, it corresponds to the sun and moon; and the excellence seen in the ease and ready response of its various operations corresponds to the perfect operations presented to us in the phenomena of nature.
The Master said:—'Is not the *Yi* a perfect book?' It was by the *Yi* that the sages exalted their virtue, and enlarged their sphere of occupation.

아는 것은 높고 예는 낮으니, 높은 것은 하늘을 본받고, 낮은 것은 땅을 본받는다. 천지天地가 자리를 설정하면 역易이 그 가운데서 행하여지니, 이루어진 본성을 보존하고 또 보존하는 것이 도의道義의 문門이다.
성인聖人은 천하의 깊은 것을 보고 그 생긴 모양을 비겨보며, 그 사물의 마땅함을 본뜬다. 이런 까닭에 일러서 상象이라 한다. 성인은 천하의 움직임을 보고 그 모이고 통함을 관찰해서 그 전례典禮를 행하며, 말을 베풀어 그 길흉을 판단한다.

Their wisdom was high, and their rules of conduct were solid. That loftiness was after the pattern of heaven; that solidity, after the pattern of earth. Heaven and earth having their positions as assigned to them, the changes of nature take place between them. The nature of man having been completed, and being continually preserved, it is the gate of all good courses and righteousness.
The sage was able to survey all the complex phenomena under the sky. He then considered in his mind how they could be figured, and by means of the diagrams represented their material forms and their character. Hence these diagrams are denominated Semblances or emblematic figures, the Xiang. A later sage was able to survey the motive influences working all under the sky. He contemplated them in their common action and special nature, in order to bring out the standard and proper tendency of each. He then appended his explanation to each line of the diagrams, to determine the good or evil indicated by it.

●鳴鶴、在陰、其子和之、我有好爵、吾與爾靡之。子曰君子居其室、出其言、善、則千里之外應之、況其邇者乎。居其室、出其言、不善、則千里之外違之、況其邇者乎。言出乎身、加乎民、行發乎邇、見乎遠、言行、君子之樞機。樞機之發、榮辱之主也、言行、君子之所以動天地也、可不愼乎。

●同人、先號咷而後笑。子曰君子之道、或出或處、或默或語。二人、同心、其利斷金、同心之言、其臭如蘭。

●初六藉用白茅、无咎。子曰苟錯諸地、而可矣、藉之用茅、何咎之有愼之至也。夫茅之爲物、薄而用、可重也。愼斯術也、以往、其无所失矣。

○勞謙、君子有終、吉。子曰、勞而不伐、有功而不德、厚之至也。語以其功下人者也。德言盛、禮言恭、謙也者、致恭、以存其位者也。

●亢龍、有悔。子曰貴而无位、高而无民、賢人在下位而无輔、是以動而有悔也。○不出戶庭、无咎。子曰亂之所生也、則言語以爲階。君不密則失臣、臣不密則失身、幾事不密則害成。是以君子愼密而不出也。

이런 까닭에 일러서 효爻라고 한다. 천하의 지극히 깊은 이치를 말하되 싫어하지 않으며, 천하에 지극한 움직임을 말하되 혼란스럽지 않다. 비겨본 뒤에 말하고 따져본 뒤에 움직이니, 비겨보고 따져보아서 그 변화를 이룬다.
우는 학鶴이 그늘에 있으니, 그 새끼가 화답한다. 내가 좋은 벼슬을 가져서 너와 함께 나눈다 하니, 공자孔子가 말씀하시길, 군자가 그 집에 살면서 말을 함에 선善하면, 천리 밖에서도 응應하니 하물며 그 가까운데 있는 사람에게 있어서랴!

Hence those lines with their explanations are denominated Imitations the Yao. The diagrams speak of the most complex phenomena under the sky, and yet there is nothing in them that need awaken dislike; the explanations of the lines speak of the subtlest movements under the sky, and yet there is nothing in them to produce confusion. A learner will consider what is said under the diagrams, and then speak; he will deliberate on what is said in the explanations of the lines, and then move. By such consideration and deliberations he will be able to make all the changes which he undertakes successful.
Here hid, retired, cries out the crane; Her young's responsive cry sounds there. Of spirits good I drain this cup; With thee a cup I'll freely share.' The Master said:— 'The superior man occupies his apartment and sendsforth his words. If they be good, they will be responded to at a distance of more than a thousand li;—how much more will they be so in the nearer circle! He occupies his apartment and sends forth his words.

그 방에 거해서 말을 함에 선하지 않으면, 천리 밖에서 어기나니, 하물며 그 가까운 데에서랴! 말이 내 몸에서 나와 백성에게 주어지며, 행실이 가까운데서 발하여 먼 데에서 나타나니, 언행은 군자의 지도리다. 지도리의 움직임이 영욕榮辱의 주인이다. 언행은 군자가 이로써 천하를 움직이니, 삼가지 않을 수 있겠는가? 사람과 함께 함이 먼저는 울지만 뒤에는 웃는다고 하니, 공자가 말씀하시길, 군자의 도道는 혹 나가기도 하고 혹 거처하기도 하며, 혹 침묵하고 혹 말하기도 하지만, 두 사람의 마음이 같으니, 그 날카로움이 쇠를 끊는다. 한 마음으로 하는 말은 그 향기가 난초와 같나.

If they be evil, they will awaken opposition at a distance of more than a thousand li;—how much more will they do so in the nearer circle! Words issue from one's person, and proceed to affect the people. Actions proceed from what is near, and their effects are seen at a distance. Words and actions are the hinge and spring of the superior man. The movement of that hinge and spring determines glory or disgrace. His words and actions move heaven and earth;—may he be careless in regard to them?'
'The representative of the union of men first cries out and weeps, and afterwards laughs.' The Master said, on this:—'The ways of good man. different seem. This in a public office toils; That in his home the time beguiles. One man his lips with silence seals; Another all his mind reveals. But when two men are one in heart, Not iron bolts keep them apart; The words they in their union use, Fragrance like orchid plants diffuse.'

초6은 까는데 흰 띠를 쓰니 허물이 없다고 하니, 공자가 말씀하시길, 그냥 땅에 놓더라도 괜찮거늘 까는데 띠를 쓰니 무슨 허물이 있겠는가? 삼가함이 지극하다. 흰띠란 사물은 하잘 것 없지만 그 쓰임은 소중하다. 이 방법을 삼가서 행하면 잘못되는 바가 없을 것이다. 겸손에 힘쓰니, 군자에게 마침이 있어서 길하다 하니, 공자가 말씀하시길, 수고로와도 자랑하지 아니하며, 공功이 있어도 덕德으로 여기지 않는 것은 지극히 후덕한 것이다. 그 공功이 있으면서 남보다 낮추는 자를 말한 것이다. 덕은 성대해야 하고 예는 공손해야 하니,

'F6, divided, shows its subject placing mats of the white grass beneath what he sets on the ground.' The Master said:— 'To place the things on the ground might be considered sufficient; but when he places beneath them mats of the white grass, what occasion for blame can there be? Such a course shows the height of carefulness. The white grass is a trivial thing, but, through the use made of it, it may become important. He who goes forward using such careful art will not fall into any error.' A superior man toiling laboriously and yet humble! He will bring things to an end, and with good fortune.' The Master said on this:— 'He toils with success, but does not boast of it; he achieves merit, but takes no virtue to himself from it;—this is the height of generous goodness, and speaks of the man who with great merit yet places himself below others. He wishes his virtue to be more and more complete, and in his intercourse with others to be more and more respectful;

겸손이란 것은 공손함을 이루어 그 자리를 보존하는 것이다. 높은 용龍은 후회가 있다 하니, 공자가 말씀하시길, 귀하여도 자리가 없으며, 높아도 백성이 없으며, 어진 사람이 아랫자리에 있어도 도움이 없다. 이로써 움직이면 후회가 있다. 문뜰을 나가지 않으면 허물이 없다고 하니, 공자가 말씀하시길, 혼란이 생기는 것은 말이 원인이 되는 것이니, 임금이 주밀하지 않으면 신하를 잃고, 신하가 주밀하지 않으면 몸을 잃으며, 기밀을 지켜야 할 일에 주밀하지 않으면 해가 되나니, 이로써 군자는 삼가고 주밀해서 나가지 않는다.

—he who is so humble, carrying his respectfulness to the utmost, will be able to preserve himself in his position.'
'The dragon is seen beyond his proper haunts; there will be occasion for repentance.' The Master said on this:— 'He is noble, but is not in his correct place; he is on high, but there are no people to acknowledge him; there is a man of virtue and ability below, but he will not assist him. Hence whatever movement he may make will give occasion for repentance.'
'He does not quit the courtyard before his door;—there will be no occasion for blame.' The Master said on this:— 'When disorder arises, it will be found that ill-advised speech was the steppingstone to it. If a ruler do not keep secret his deliberations with his minister, he will lose that minister. If a minister do not keep secret his deliberations with his ruler, he will lose his life. If important matters in the germ be not kept secret, that will be injurious to their accomplishment. Therefore the superior man is careful to maintain secrecy, and dose not allow himself to speak.'

공자가 말씀하시길, 역易을 지은 이는 그 도적을 알 것인저! 역易에서 말하기를, 짐을 지고 또 수레를 타니, 도적이 이르게 된다고 하니, 지는 것은 소인이 일이요, 타는 것은 군자의 기물이니, 소인이 군자의 기물을 타는 것이다. 도적은 빼앗을 것을 생각하며, 위에서 거만하게 하고 아래에서 사납게 하니, 도적이 칠 것을 생각한다. 태만히 간수하는 것이 도적을 가르치는 것이며, 얼굴을 꾸미는 것이 음탕함을 가르치는 것이니, 역易에 말하기를, 짐을 지고 또 수레를 타니 도적이 이르게 된다고 하니, 이는 도적을 부르는 것이다.
하늘은 하나요, 땅은 둘이며, 하늘은 셋이요 땅은 넷이며, 하늘은 다섯이요 땅은 여섯이며, 하늘은 일곱이요 땅은 여덟이며, 하늘은 아홉이며 땅은 열이다.

The Master said:— 'The makers of the Yi may be said to have known the philosophy of robbery. The Yi says, "He is a burden-bearer, and yet rides in a carriage, thereby exciting robbers to attack him." Burden-bearing is the business of a small man. A carriage is the vehicle of a gentleman. When a small man rides in the vehicle of a gentleman, robbers will think of taking it from him. When one is insolent to those above him, and oppressive to those below, robbers will wish to attack him. Careless laying up of things excites to robbery, as a woman's adorning of herself excites to lust. What the Yi says about the burdenbearer's riding in a carriage, and exciting robbers to attack him, shows how robbery is called out.'
To heaven belongs the number 1; to earth, 2; to heaven, 3; to earth, 4; to heaven, 5; to earth, 6; to heaven, 7; to earth, 8; to heaven, 9; to earth, 10.

●子曰作易者其知盜乎 易曰負且乘、致寇至。負也者、小人之事也、乘也者、君子之器也。小人而乘君子之器、盜思奪之矣、上、慢、下、暴、盜思伐之矣。慢藏、誨盜、治容、誨淫。易曰「負且乘致寇至」、盜之招也。

(以上 第八章)

●天一地二天三地四天五地六天七地八天九地十。○天數五、地數五、五位相得、而各有合。天數二十有五、地數三十、凡天地之數五十有五。此所以成變化、而行鬼神也。○大衍之數五十、其用、四十有九。分而爲二、以象兩、掛一、以象三、揲之以四、以象四時、歸奇於扐、以象閏、五歲、再閏、故、再扐而後、掛。

●乾之策、二百一十有六、坤之策、百四十有四、凡三百有六十、當期之日。○二篇之策、萬有一千五百二十、當萬物之數也。○是故、四營而成易、十有八變而成卦、○八卦而小成。○引而伸之、觸類而長之、天下之能事畢矣。○顯道、神德行、是故、可與酬酢、可與祐神矣。○子曰知變化之道者、其知神之所爲乎。

(以上 第九章)

하늘의 수數가 다섯이요, 땅의 수數가 다섯이니, 다섯 자리가 서로 얻어서 각각 합함이 있으니, 하늘 수數가 이십오二十五요, 땅의 수數가 삼십三十이니, 무릇 천지의 수가 오십오五十五이다. 이것이 변화를 이루며 귀신을 부리는 까닭이다. 크게 푸는 수數는 오십五十이나 그 씀은 사십구四十九이다. 나누어서 둘로 하여 양의를 본뜨고, 하나를 손가락 사이에 걸어서 셋(三才)을 본뜨고, 넷씩 세어서 사시四時를 본뜨고, 나머지를 손가락 사이에 끼워서 윤달을 본뜨고, 오년五年 만에 두 번 윤달이니, 그러므로 다시 끼운 후에 건다.

The numbers belonging to heaven are five, and those belonging to earth are also five. The numbers of there two series correspond to each other in their fixed positions, and each one has another that may be considered its mate. The heavenly numbers amount to 25, and the earthly to 30. The numbers of heaven and earth together amount to 55. It is by these that the changes and transformations are effected, and the spirit-like agencies kept in movement. The numbers of the Great Expansion, multiplied together, make 50, of which only 49 are used in divination. The stalks representing these are divided into two heaps to represent the two emblematic lines, or heaven and earth. One is then taken from the heap on the right, and placed between the little finger of the left hand and the next, that there may thus be symbolised the three powers of heaven, earth, and man. The heaps on both sides are manipulated by fours to represent the four seasons; and then the remainders are returned, and placed between the two middle fingers of the left hand, to represent the intercalary month. In five years there are two intercalations, and therefore there are two operations; and afterwards the whole process is repeated.

건乾의 책수策數는 216이요, 곤坤의 책수策數는 144이다. 무릇 360이니 1년의 날수에 해당하고, 두 편(주역의 상·하경)의 책수策數가 11,520이니 만물의 수에 해당한다. 이런 까닭에 네 번씩 운영해서 역易을 이루고, 18번 변해서 괘卦를 이루니, 팔괘八卦로 작게 이룬다. 이끌어펴서 종류를 더듬어 펴나가면, 천지의 가능한 일을 다한다. 도를 밝히고 덕행을 신비롭게 하니, 이런 까닭에 신과 더불어 응대하고 신을 도울 수 있다. 공자가 말씀하시길, 변화의 도를 아는 자는 신이 하는 바를 알고 있을 것이라 하였다.

The numbers required for *Qian* or the undivided line amount to 216; those for *Kun* or the divided line, to 144. Together they are 360, corresponding to the days of the year. The number produced by the lines in the two parts of the *Yi* amount to 11,520, corresponding to the number of all things. Therefore by means of the four operations is the *Yi* completed. It takes 18 changes to form a hexagram. The formation of the eight trigrams constitutes the small completion of the *Yi*. If we lad on the diagrams and expanded them, if we prolonged each by the addition of the proper lines, then all events possible under the sky might have their representation. The diagrams make manifest by their appended explanations, the ways of good and ill fortune, and show virtuous actions in their spiritual relations. In this way, by consulting them, we may receive an answer to our doubts, and we may also by means of them assist the spiritual power in its agency in nature and providence. The Master said:—'He who knows the method of change and transformation may be said to know what is done by that spiritual power.'

역易에 성인聖人의 도道가 네가지 있으니, 말로써 하는 자는 그 말을 숭상하고, 행동으로써 하는 자는 그 변함을 숭상하고, 기물을 짓는 자는 그 상象을 숭상하고, 복서卜筮로써 하는 자는 그 점을 숭상한다. 이로써 군자가 장차 할 일이 있으며, 장차 행할 일이 있을 때 말로써 묻거든, 그 명을 받음이 메아리가 울리는 것 같아, 멀고 가깝고 어둡고 깊음이 없으니, 드디어 오는 사물을 알게 된다. 천하의 지극한 정미로움이 아니면 그 누가 여기에 참여할 수 있겠는가?

In the *Yi* there are four things characteristic of the way of the sages. We should set the highest value on its explanations to guide us in speaking; on its changes for the initiation of our movement; on its emblematic figures for definite action as in the construction of implement; and on its prognostications for our practice of divination. Therefore, when a superior man is about to take action of a more private or of a public character, he asks the *Yi*, making his inquiry in words. It receives his order, and the answer comes as the echo's response. Be the subject remote or near, mysterious or deep, he forthwith knows of what kind will be the coming result. If the *Yi* were not the most exquisite thing under heaven, would it be concerned in such an operation as this? The stalks are manipulated by threes and fives to determine one change; they are laid on opposite sides, and placed one up, one down, to make sure of their numbers; and the three necessary changes are gone through with in this way, till they form the figures pertaining to heaven or to earth. Their numbers are exactly determined, and the emblems of all things under the sky are fixed. If the *Yi* were not the thing most capable of change of all things under heaven, how could it effect such a result as this?

●易有聖人之道四焉、以言者、尚其辭、以動者、尚其變、以制器者、尚其象、以卜筮者、尚其占。○是以君子將有爲也、將有行也、問焉而以言、其受命也如嚮、无有遠近幽深、遂知來物。非天下之至精、其孰能與於此。

●參伍以變、錯綜其數、通其變、遂成天下之文、極其數、遂定天下之象。非天下之至變、其孰能與於此。○易、无思也、无爲也、寂然不動、感而遂通天下之故。非天下之至神、其孰能與於此。○夫易、聖人之所以極深而研幾也。○唯深也故、能通天下之志、唯幾也故、能成天下之務、唯神也故、不疾而速、不行而至。子曰易有聖人之道四焉者、此之謂也。（以上 第十章）

●子曰夫易何爲者也。夫易、開物成務、冒天下之道、如斯而已者也。是故、聖人以通天下之志、以定天下之業、以斷天下之疑。○是故、蓍之德、圓而神、卦之德、方以知、六爻之義、易以貢。聖人、以此、洗心、退藏於密、吉凶、與民同患、神以知來、如以藏往。其孰能與於此哉。古之聰明叡智、神武而不殺者夫。

셋과 다섯으로 변하며, 그 수를 착종하여 그 변함을 통해서 드디어 천지의 무늬를 이루고, 그 수를 다해서 드디어 천하의 상象을 정한다. 천하의 지극한 변화가 아니면 그 누가 여기에 참여할 수 있겠는가? 역易은 생각함도 없고 행위하는 것도 없으며, 고요히 움직이지 않다가, 느껴서 드디어 천하의 연고緣故에 통하니, 천하의 지극한 신묘함이 아니면 그 누가 여기에 참여할 수 있겠는가? 대저 역易은 성인이 깊이 이치를 다하고 기미를 연구한 바니 오직 심오하다. 그러므로 천하의 뜻에 통할 수 있다. 오직 미묘하므로 천하의 일거리를 이룰 수 있으며, 오직 신령한 고로 달리지 않아도 빠르며 가지 않아도 이른다. 공자가 말씀하시길, 역易에 성인의 도道가 넷이 있다 함은 이것을 말한 것이라 하였다.

In all these operations forming the *Yi*, there is no thought and no action. It is still and without movement; but, when acted on, it penetrates forthwith to all phenomena and events under the sky. If it were not the most spirit-like thing under the sky, how could it be found doing this? The operations forming the *Yi* are the method by which the sages searched out exhaustively what was deep, and investigated the minutest springs of things. 'Those operations searched out what was deep;—therefore they could penetrate to the views of all under th sky. 'They made apparent the minutest springs of things:'—therefore they could bring to a completion all undertakings under the sky. 'Their action was spirit-like:'—therefore they could make speed without hurry, and reached their destination without travelling. This is the import of what the Master said, that 'In the *Yi* there are four things indicating the way of the sages.'

공자가 말씀하시길, 역易은 무엇인가? 대저 역易은 사물을 개화開化시켜 일을 이루며, 천하의 도道를 덮으니 이와 같을 뿐이다. 이런 까닭에 성인은 이로써 천하의 뜻을 통하고 천하의 사업을 정하며, 천하의 의문을 끊는다. 이런 까닭에 시초蓍草의 덕은 둥글어서 신령스럽고, 괘卦의 덕은 반듯해서 지혜롭고, 육효六爻의 의의는 바뀌서 알려준다. 성인이 이로써 마음을 닦아서 물러나 은밀한 데 감추며, 길흉에 백성과 더불어 한가지로 근심하여, 신묘하게 오는 것을 알고 지혜로서 감추고 간다. 그 누가 능히 이에 참여하겠는가?

The Master said :—'What is it that the *Yi* dose? The *Yi* opens up the knowledge of the issues of things, accomplishes the undertakings of men, and embraces under it the way of all things under the sky. This and nothing more is what the *Yi* dose. Thereby the sages, through divination by it, would give their proper course to the aims of all under the sky, would give stability to their undertakings, and determine their doubts.' Therefore the virtue of the stalks is versatile and spirit-like; that of the diagrams is exact and wise; and the meaning given by the six lines is changeful to give the proper information to men. The sages having, by their possession of these three virtues, cleansed their minds, retired and laid them up in the secrecy of their own consciousness. But their sympathies were with the people in regard both to their good fortune and evil. By their spirit-like ability they knew the character of coming events, and their wisdom had stored up all experiences of the past. Who could be able to accomplish all this?

옛날의 총명하고 예지를 갖고 있으며, 신묘한 무예를 지녔으나, 사람을 죽이지 않는 자일 것이다.
이로써 하늘의 도를 밝히고 백성의 사정을 살펴서, 이에 신물神物을 일으켜 백성이 쓰는데 앞세운다. 성인이 이로써 재계하여 그 덕을 신명하게 할 것이다. 이런 까닭에 문門을 닫은 것을 곤坤이라 이르고, 문을 연 것을 건乾이라 이르며, 한번 닫고 한번 여는 것을 변화라고 이르고, 가고 오는 데 궁하지 않은 것을 통함이라 이르며, 나타난 것을 상象이라 이르고,

Only our ancient sages, quick in apprehension and clear in discernment, of far-reaching intelligence, and all-embracing knowledge, and with a majesty, going spirit-like to its objects; —it was only they who could do so.
Therefore those sages, fully understanding the way of Heaven, and having clearly ascertained the experience of the people, instituted the employment of these spirit-like things, as a provision for the use of the people. The sages went about the employment of them moreover by purifying their hearts and with reverent caution, thereby giving more spirituality and intelligence to their virtue. Thus, a door shut may be pronounced analogous to *Kun* or the inactive condition, and the opening of the door analogous to *Qian* or the active condition. The opening succeeding the being shut may be pronounced analogous to what we call a change; and the passing from one of these states to the other may be called the constant course of things. The first appearance of anything as a bud is what we call a semblance; when it has received its complete form, we call it a definite thing.

●是以明於天之道而察於民之故、是興神物、以前民用。聖人、以此齊戒、以神明其德夫。○是故、闔戶、謂之坤、闢戶、謂之乾、一闔一闢、謂之變、往來不窮、謂之通、見、乃謂之象、形乃謂之器、制而用之、謂之法、利用出入、民咸用之、謂之神。

●是故、易有太極、是生兩儀、兩儀生四象、四象生八卦、○八卦定吉凶、吉凶、生大業。○是故、法象、莫大乎天地、變通、莫大乎四時、縣象著明、莫大乎日月、崇高莫大乎富貴、備物、致用、立成器、以爲天下利、莫大乎聖人。探賾索隱、鉤深致遠、以定天下之吉凶、成天下之亹亹者、莫大乎蓍龜。

●是故、天生神物、聖人、則之、天地變化、聖人、效之、天垂象、見吉凶、聖人、象之、河出圖、洛出書、聖人、則之。○易有四象、所以示也、繫辭焉、所以告也、定之以吉凶、所以斷也。（以上 第十一章）

형용이 있는 것을 기器라 이르며, 만들어서 쓰는 것을 법法이라 이르고, 이롭게 써서 드나들며 백성이 다 쓰는 것을 신神이라 이른다.
이런 까닭에 역易에는 태극太極이 있으니, 이것이 양의兩儀를 낳고, 양의는 사상四象을 낳고, 사상은 팔괘八卦를 낳으니 팔괘는 길흉을 정하고 길흉은 대업大業을 낳는다. 이런 까닭에 본뜬 상이 천지보다 크지 않고, 변하여 통하는 것은 사시四時보다 크지 않으며, 형상을 드러내고 밝은 것을 나타내는 것은 일월日月보다 크지 않고,

The divining-plant having been produced, the sages set it apart and laid down the method of its employment,—what we call the laws of divination. The advantage arising from it in external and internal matters, so that the people all use it, stamps it with a character which we call spirit-like.
Therefore in the system of the *Yi* there is the Grand Terminus, which produced the two elementary Forms. Those two Forms produced the Four emblematic Symbols, which again produced the eight Trigrams. The eight trigrams served to determine the good and evil issues of events, and from this determination was produced the successful prosecution of the great business of life. Therefore of all things that furnish models and visible figures there are none greater than heaven and earth; of things that change and extend an influence on others there are none greater than the four seasons; of things suspended in the sky with their figures displayed clear and bright, there are none greater than the sun and moon;

숭고하기로는 부귀보다 큰 것이 없으며, 사물을 갖추어 쓰게 하고, 형상을 세우고 기물을 만들어 천하를 이롭게 함은 성인보다 크지 않다. 깊은 이치를 탐구하여 은밀한 것을 찾으며, 깊이 있는 것을 끌어내고 멀리있는 것에 이르게 하여 천하의 길흉을 정하며, 천하 사람들이 힘써 노력하는 것을 이루는 것으로는 시구蓍龜보다 큰 것은 없다.
이런 까닭에 하늘이 신물神物을 낳으니 성인이 그것을 본받고, 천지가 변화하니 성인이 그것을 본받으며, 하늘이 상을 드리워서 길흉을 나타내니 성인이 그것을 본뜨며,

of the honoured and exalted there are none greater than he who is the rich and noble one; in preparing things for practical use, and inventing and making instruments for the benefit of all under the sky, there are none greater than the sages; to explore what is complex, search out what is hidden, to hook up what lies deep, and reach to what is distant, thereby determining the issues for good or ill of all events under the sky, and making all men under heaven full of strenuous endeavours, there are no agencies greater than those of the stalks and the tortoise-shell.
Therefore Heaven produced the spirit-like things, and the sages took advantage of them. The operations of heaven and earth are marked by so many changes and transformations; and the sages imitated them by means of the *Yi*. Heaven hangs out its brilliant figures from which are seen good fortune and bad, and the sages made their emblematic interpretations accordingly.

하수河水에서 하도河圖가 나오고 낙수洛水에서 낙서落書가 나오니, 성인이 그것을 본받는다. 역易에 사상四象이 있음을 보이고, 말에 매여서 알려주며, 길흉으로 정해서 판단하게 한다.
역易에 말하기를, 하늘로부터 도우니 길하여 이롭지 않음이 없다고 하니, 공자가 말씀하시길, 우祐는 돕는 것이니 하늘은 따르는 사람을 돕고, 사람은 미더운 사람을 도우니, 믿음을 실천하고 순조로움을 생각하며 또 현명한 사람을 숭상한다. 이로써 하늘로부터 도와서 길하여 이롭지 않음이 없다.

The He gave forth the map, and the Luo the writing, of both of which the sages took advantage.
In the scheme of the *Yi* there are the four symbolic figures by which they inform men in divining of the lines making up the diagrams; the explanations appended to them convey the significance of the diagrams and lines; and the determination of the divination as fortunate or the reverse, to settle the doubts of men.
It is said in the *Yi*, 'Help is given to him from Heaven. There will be good fortune; advantage in every respect.' The Master said:—'You is the symbol of assisting. He Whom Heaven assists is observant of what is right; he whom men assist is sincere. The individual here indicated treads the path of sincerity and desires to be observant of what is right, and studies to exalt the worthy. Hence "Help is given to him from Heaven. There will be good fortune, advantage in every respect."'

●易曰、自天祐之、吉无不利。子曰、祐者、助也。天之所助者順也、人之所助者信也。履信思乎順、又以尚賢也、是以自天祐之吉无不利也。○子曰、書不盡言、言不盡意。然則聖人之意、其不可見乎？子曰、聖人、立象、以盡意、設卦、以盡情僞、繫辭焉、以盡其言、變而通之、以盡利、鼓之舞之、以盡神。

●乾坤、其易之縕邪。乾坤、成列而易、立乎其中矣、乾坤、毀則无以見易、易、不可見則乾坤、或幾乎息矣。○是故、形而上者、謂之道、形而下者、謂之器、化而裁之、謂之變、推而行之、謂之通、擧而錯之天下之民、謂之事業。

●是故、夫象、聖人、有以見天下之賾、而擬諸其形容、象其物宜、是故謂之象。聖人、有以見天下之動、而觀其會通、以行其曲禮、繫辭焉、以斷其吉凶、是故謂之爻。○極天下之賾者、存乎卦、鼓天下之動者、存乎辭、○化而裁之、存乎變、推而行之、存乎通、神而明之存乎其人、默而成之、不言而信、存乎德行。(以上 第十二章)

공자가 말씀하시길, 글로는 말을 다하지 못하고, 말로는 뜻을 다하지 못하니, 그런즉 성인의 뜻을 볼 수 없겠는가? 공자가 말씀하시길, 성인이 상象을 세워서 뜻을 다하고, 괘卦를 베풀어서 참과 거짓을 다하며, 말을 지어서 그 할 말을 다하고, 변하고 통하게 해서 이로움을 다하며, 두드리고 춤춰서 신묘함을 다하도록 하였다.
건乾과 곤坤은 그 역易의 핵심인가? 건과 곤이 펼쳐짐에 역易이 그 가운데 서니, 건곤이 훼손되면 역을 볼 수 없고, 역을 보지 못하면 건곤의 작용이 거의 끝나게 된다.

The Master said:—'The written characters are not the full exponent of speech, and speech is not the full expression of ideas; —is it impossible then to discover the ideas of the sages?' The Master said:—'The sages made their emblematic symbols to set forth fully their ideas; appointed all the diagrams to show fully the truth and falsehood of things; appended their explanations to give the full expression of their words; and changed the various lines and made general the method of doing so, to exhibit fully what was advantageous. They thus stimulated the people as by drums and dances, thereby completely developing the spirit-like character of the *Yi*.
May we not say that *Qian* and *Kun*, or the undivided and divided lines are the secret and substance of the *Yi*? *Qian* and *Kun* being established in their several places, the system of changes was thereby constituted. If *Qian* and *Kun* were taken away, there would be no means of seeing that system; and if that system were not seen, *Qian* and *Kun* would almost cease to act.

이런 까닭에 형체 너머에 있는 것을 도道라고 이르고, 형체 아래에 있는 것을 기器라 이르며, 변화하여 조절하는 것을 변變이라 이르고, 미루어 행하는 것을 통通이라 이르며, 이를 들어서 천하의 백성에 베푸는 것을 사업事業이라 이른다.
이런 까닭에 대저 상象은 성인이 천하의 잡다한 것을 보아서 그 모습을 비기며 사물의 마땅함을 본뜨니, 이런 까닭에 상象이라 이름한다. 성인이 천하의 움직임을 보아서 그 모이고 통함을 관찰하여 그 법도를 행하며, 말을 베풀어 그 길흉을 판단하니,

Hence that which is antecedent to the material form exists, we say, as an ideal method, and that which is subsequent to the material form exists, we say, as a definite thing. Transformation and shaping is what we call change; carrying this out and operationg with it is what we call generalising the method; taking the result and setting it forth for all the people under heaven is, we say, securing the success of the business of life.
Hence, to speak of the emblematic figures:—The sage was able to survey all the complex phenomena under the sky. He then considered in his mind how they could be figured, and by means of the diagrams represented their material forms and their character. Hence those diagrams are denominated Semblances. A later sage was able to survey the motive influences working all under the sky. He contemplated them in their common action and special nature, in order to bring out the standard and proper tendency of each. He then appended his explanation to each line, to determine the good or evil indicated by it.

이런 까닭에 효爻라 이른다. 천하의 잡다함을 극진히 하는 것은 괘卦에 있고, 천하의 움직임을 고동시키는 것은 말에 있으며, 변화하여 조절하는 것은 변하는 데 있고, 미루어 행하는 것은 통하는데 달려 있으며, 신명스럽게 밝히는 것은 그 사람에 달려있고, 조용히 이루고 말하지 않아도 미더운 것은 덕행德行에 달려 있다.

Hence those lines with their explanations are denominated Imitations the *Yao*. The most thorough mastery of all the complex phenomena under the sky is obtained from the diagrams. The greatest stimulus to movement in adaptation to all affairs under the sky is obtained from the explanations. The transformations and shaping that take place are obtained from the changes of the lines; the carrying this out and operating with it is obtained from the general method that has been established. The seeing their spirit-like intimations and understanding them depended on their being the proper men; and the completing the study of them by silent meditation, and securing the faith of others without the use of words, depended on their virtuous conduct.

●八卦成列、象在其中矣、因而重之、爻在其中矣、○剛柔相推、變在其中矣、繫辭焉而命之、動在其中矣。○吉凶悔吝者、生乎動者也、○剛柔者、立本者也、變通者、趣時者也。

●吉凶者、貞勝者也、○天地之道、貞觀者也、日月之道、貞明者也、天下之動、貞夫一者也。○夫乾、確然、示人易矣、夫坤、隤然、示人簡矣。

●爻也者、效此者也、象也者、像此者也。○爻象、動乎內、吉凶、見乎外、功業、見乎變、聖人之情、見乎辭。

●天地之大德曰生、聖人之大寶曰位。何以守位？曰仁。何以聚人？曰財。理財、正辭、禁民爲非曰義。(以上第一章)

●古者包犧氏之王天下也、仰則觀象於天、俯則觀法於地、觀鳥獸之文、與地之宜、近取諸身、遠取諸物、於是、始作八卦、以通神明之德、以類萬物之情。○作結繩而爲罔罟、以佃以漁、蓋取諸離。○包犧氏沒、神農氏作、斲木爲耜、揉木爲耒、耒耨之利、以敎天下、蓋取諸益。○日中爲市、致天下之民、聚天下之貨、交易而退、各得其所、蓋取諸噬嗑。

팔괘八卦가 열을 이루니 상이 그 가운데 있고, 그로 인해 거듭하니 효가 그 가운데 있으며, 강유剛柔가 서로 밀치니 변함이 그 가운데에 있고, 말을 베풀어 명하니 움직임이 그 가운데 있다. 길하고 흉하고 후회하고 궁색한 것은 움직이는 데서 생기고, 강유는 근본을 세우는 것이며, 변통變通은 때에 나아가는 것이다.
길흉이란 바름이 이기는 것이니, 천지의 도는 바르게 보는 것이요, 해와 달의 도는 바르게 밝은 것이며, 천하의 움직임은 하나를 바르게 하는 것이다.

The eight trigrams having been completed in their proper order, there were in each the three emblematic lines. They were then multiplied by a process of addition till the six component lines appeared. The strong line and the weak push themselves each into the place of the other, and hence the changes of the diagrams take place. The appended explanations attach to every form of them its character of good or ill, and hence the movements suggested by divination are determined accordingly. Good fortune and ill, occasion for repentance or regret, all arise from these movements. The strong and the weak lines have their fixed and proper places in the diagrams; their changes, however varied, are according to the requirements of the time when they take place.
Good fortune and ill are continually prevailing each against the other by an exact rule. By the same rule, heaven and earth, in their course, continually give forth their lessons; the sun and moon continually emit their light; all the movements under the sky are constantly subject to this one and the same rule.

대저 건乾은 강건하니 사람에게 쉬운 것으로써 보임이요, 대저 곤坤은 유순하니 사람에게 간략한 것으로써 보여주니, 효爻는 이것을 본받는 것이요, 상象은 이것을 형상화한 것이다. 효와 상은 안에서 움직이고 길과 흉은 밖에서 나타나며, 공업功業은 변하는 데서 나타나고, 성인의 정은 말에서 나타난다.
천지의 큰 덕德은 생生이라 하고, 성인의 큰 보배는 자리라고 하니, 무엇으로 자리를 지킬 것인가? 인자함이라 말한다. 어떻게 사람을 모을 것인가? 재물이라고 말한다. 재물을 다스리고 말을 바르게 하며 백성의 잘못을 금하는 것을 의義라고 말한다.

Qian, the symbol of heaven, and conveying the idea of strength, shows to men its easy and natural action. *Kun*, the symbol of earth, and conveying the idea of docility, shows to men its compendious receptivity and operation. The *Yao* or lines are imitative representations of this. The *Xiang*, or emblematic figures, are pictorial representations of the same. The movements of the lines and figures take place at the hand of the operator, and are unseen; the good fortune or ill is seen openly and is beyond. The work to be done appears by the changes; the sympathies of the sages are seen in their explanations.
The great attribute of heaven and earth is the giving and maintaining life. What is most precious for the sage is to get the highest place— in which he can be the human representative of heaven and earth. What will guard this position for him? Men. How shall he collect a large population round him? By the power of his wealth. The right administration of that wealth, correct instructions to the people, and prohibitions against wrong-doing;—these constitute his righteousness.

옛날의 포희씨包犧氏가 천하를 다스릴 때 우러러서는 하늘에서 상象을 보고, 굽혀서 땅에서 법法을 관찰하며 조수의 무늬와 땅의 마땅함을 보며, 가까이로는 몸에서 취하고 멀리로는 사물에서 취하여, 이에 비로소 팔괘를 만들어서 신명神明의 덕을 통하고 이로써 만물의 실정을 유추한다. 노끈을 매서 그물을 만들어 그것으로 사냥하고 물고기를 잡으니, 대개 이괘離卦에서 취한 것이다. 포희씨가 죽으니 신농씨神農氏가 일어나 나무를 깎아 보습을 만들고 나무를 굽혀 쟁기를 만들어 쟁기의 이로움으로써 천하를 가르치니, 익괘益卦에서 취한 것이다.

Anciently, when Bao-xi had come to the rule of all under heaven, looking up, he contemplated the brilliant forms exhibited in the sky, and looking down he surveyed the patterns shown on the earth. He contemplated the ornamental appearances of birds and beasts and the different suitabilities of the soil. Near at hand, in his own person, he found things for consideration, and the same at a distance, in things in general. On this he devised the eight trigrams, to show fully the attributes of the spirit-like and intelligent operations working secretly, and to classify the qualities of the myriads of things. He invented the making of nets of various kinds by knitting strings, both for hunting and fishing. The idea of this was taken, probably, from *Li* the third trigram, and thirtieth hexagram. On the death of Bao-xi, there arose Shen-nong in his place. He fashioned wood to form the share, and bent wood to make the plough-handle. The advantages of ploughing and weeding were then taught to all under heaven. The idea of this was taken, probably, from *Yi* the forty-second hexagram.

●神農氏沒、黃帝堯舜氏作、通其變、使民不倦、神而化之、使民宜之。易、窮則變、變則通、通則久、是以自天祐之、吉无不利。黃帝堯舜、垂衣裳而天下治、蓋取諸乾坤。○刳木爲舟、剡木爲楫、舟楫之利、以濟不通、致遠以利天下、蓋取諸渙。○服牛乘馬、引重致遠、以利天下、蓋取諸隨。

●重門擊柝、以待暴客、蓋取諸豫。○斷木爲杵、掘地爲臼、臼杵之利、萬民、以濟、蓋取諸小過。○弦木爲弧、剡木爲矢、弧矢之利、以威天下、蓋取諸睽。

●上古、穴居而野處、後世聖人、易之以宮室、上棟下宇、以待風雨、蓋取諸大壯。○古之葬者、厚衣之以薪、葬之中野、不封不樹、喪期无數、後世聖人、易之以棺槨、蓋取諸大過。○上古、結繩而治、後世聖人、易之以書契、百官以治、萬民、以察、蓋取諸夬。（以上 第二章）

●是故、易者、象也、象也者、像也。○彖者、材也、○爻也者、效天下之動者也。○是故、吉凶、生而悔吝、著也。（以上 第三章）

한낮에 시장을 만들어 천하의 백성이 이르게 하며 천하의 재물을 모아서 서로 교역하게 하여 각기 그 갈 곳을 얻게 하니, 대개 서합괘噬嗑卦에서 취한 것이다.
신농씨가 죽으니 황제黃帝·요堯·순舜씨가 나와서, 그 변화를 통하게 해서 백성으로 하여금 게으르지 않게 했으며, 신묘하게 교화하여 백성으로 하여금 마땅하게 하였다. 역易이 궁하면 변하고, 변하면 통하고, 통하면 오래간다. 이로써 하늘로부터 도우니 길하여 이롭지 않음이 없다. 황제·요·순이 의상衣裳을 드리우고 천하를 다스리니,

He caused markets to be held at midday, thus bringing together all the people, and assembling in one place all their wares. They made their exchanges and retired, every one having got what he wanted. The idea of this was taken, probably, from *Shike* the twenty-first hexagram.
After the death of Shen-nong, there arose *Huang di*, *Yao*, and *Shun*. They carried through the necessarily occurring changes, so that the people did what was required of them without being wearied; yea, they exerted such a spirit-like transformation, that the people felt constrained to approve their ordinances as right. When a series of changes has run all its course, another change ensues. When it obtains free course, it will continue long. Hence it was that 'these sovereigns were helped by Heaven; they had good fortune, and their every movement was advantageous.' *Huang di*, *Yao*, and *Shun* simply wore their upper and lower garments as patterns to the people, and good order was secured all under heaven.

대개 건곤괘乾坤卦에서 취한 것이다. 나무를 잘라서 배를 만들고, 나무를 깎아 노를 만들며, 배와 노의 이로움으로써 통하지 못하는 곳을 건너게 하여, 먼 곳에 이르게 하여 천하를 이롭게 하니, 대개 환괘渙卦에서 취한 것이다. 소를 길들이고 말을 타서, 무거운 것을 끌고 먼 곳에 이르게 하여 천하를 이롭게 하니, 대개 수괘隨卦에서 취한 것이다.
문을 겹으로 닫고 목탁을 쳐서 도적을 대비하니 대개 저 예괘豫卦에서 취한 것이다. 나무를 잘라서 공이를 만들고 땅을 파서 절구를 만들어

The idea of all this was taken, probably, from *Qian* and *Kun* the first and eighth trigrams, or the first and second hexagrams. They hollowed out trees to form canoes; they cut others long and thin to make oars. Thus arose the benefit of canoes and oars for the help of those who had no means of intercourse with others. They could now reach the most distant parts, and all under heaven were benefited. The idea of this was taken, probably, from *Huan* the fifty-ninth hexagram. They used oxen in carts and yoked horses to chariots, thus providing for the carriage of what was heavy, and for distant journeys,—thereby benefiting all under the sky. The idea of this was taken, probably, from *Sui* the seventeenth hexagram.
They made the defence of the double gates, and the warning of the clapper, as a preparation against the approach of marauding visitors. The idea of this was taken, probably, from *Yu* the sixteenth hexagram. They cut wood and fashioned it into pestles; they dug in the ground and formed mortars.

절구와 공이의 이로움으로 만민을 구제하니, 대개 소과괘小過卦에서 취한 것이다. 나무를 휘어 활을 만들고, 나무를 깎아서 화살을 만들어, 활과 화살의 날카로움으로써 천하에 위엄을 보이니, 대개 규괘睽卦에서 취한 것이다.
옛날에는 토굴에서 살고 들에 거처하더니, 후세에 성인이 집으로써 바꾸고, 위로 기둥을 세우고 아래로 지붕을 얹어서 바람과 비를 막으니, 대개 대장괘大壯卦에서 취한 것이다. 옛날의 장사는 섶나무로써 두텁게 싸서, 들판 가운데서 장사를 지내되, 봉분을 하지 않고, 묻지도 않으며 복상의 기간이 일정치 않았는데,

Thus the myriads of the people received the benefit arising from the use of the pestle and mortar. The idea of this was taken, probably, from *Xiaoguo* the sixty-second hexagram. They bent wood by means of string so as to form bows, and sharpened wood so as to make arrows. This gave the benefit of bows and arrows, and served to produce everywhere a feeling of awe. The idea of this was taken, probably, from *Kui* the thirty-eighth hexagram.
In the highest antiquity they made their homes in winter in caves, and in summer dwelt in the open country. In subsequent ages, for these the sages substituted houses, with the ridge-beam above and the projecting roof below, as a provision against wind and rain. The idea of this was taken, probably, from Ta *Dazhuang* the thirty-fourth hexagram. When the ancients buried their dead, they covered the body thickly with pieces of wood, having laid it in the open country. They raised no mound over it, nor planted trees around; nor had they any fixed period for mourning.

후세에 성인이 관락棺槨으로써 바꾸니 대개 대과괘大過卦에서 취한 것이다. 옛날에는 노끈을 맺어서 다스리더니, 후세에 성인이 글로써 바꾸니, 백관이 다스려지고 만민이 살펴지니, 대개 쾌괘夬卦에서 취한 것이다.
이런 까닭에 역易이란 상象이니, 상象이란 것은 본뜨는 것이다. 단彖이란 재질이요, 효爻란 천하의 움직임을 본받은 것이다. 이런 까닭에 길흉이 생기고 회린이 나타난다.

In subsequent ages the sages substituted for these practices the inner and outer coffins. The idea of this was taken, probably, from *Daguo* the twenty-eighth hexagram. In the highest antiquity, government was carried on successfully by the use of knotted cords to preserve the memory of things. In subsequent ages the sages substituted for these written characters and bonds. By means of these the doings of all the officers could be regulated, and the affairs of all the people accurately examined. The idea of this was taken, probably, from *Guai* the forty-third hexagram.
Therefore what we call the *Yi* is a collection of emblematic lines. They are styled emblematic as being resemblances. What we call the *Tuan* or king Wan's explanations are based on the significance of each hexagram as a whole. We call the lines of the figures *Yao* from their being according to the movements taking place all under the sky. In this way we see the rise of good fortune and evil, and the manifestation of repentance and regret.

양괘陽卦는 음陰이 많고 음괘陰卦는 양陽이 많으니, 그 까닭은 무엇인가? 양괘는 홀수요 음괘는 짝수이니, 그 덕행은 무엇인가? 양陽은 한 임금에 두 백성이니 군자의 도道요, 음陰은 두 임금에 한 백성이니 소인의 도道이다.

역易에서 말하기를, 자주 가고 오면 벗이 네 생각을 따른다고 하니, 공자가 말씀하기를, 천하에 무엇을 생각하고 무엇을 염려하는가? 천하는 돌아가는 곳은 같아도 가는 길은 다르며, 이루는 것은 하나지만 생각은 백가지이니, 천하에 무엇을 생각하며 무엇을 염려하는가?

In the *Yang* trigrams or those of the undivided line there are more of the *Yin* lines, and in the *Yin* trigrams or those of the divided line there are more of the *Yang* lines. What is the cause of this? It is because the *Yang* lines are odd or made by one stroke, and the *Yin* lines are even or made by two strokes. What method of virtuous conduct is thus intimated? In the *Yang* trigrams we have one ruler, and two subjects,—suggesting the way of the superior man. In the *Yin* trigrams we have two rulers, and one subject,—suggesting the way of the small man.

It is said in the *Yi*, 'Full of anxious thoughts you go and come; only friends will follow you and think with you.' The Master said:—'In all the processes taking place under heaven, what is there of thinking? what is there of anxious scheming? They all come to the same successful issue, though by different paths; there is one result, though there might be a hundred anxious schemes. What is there of thinking? what is there of anxious scheming?'

●陽卦、多陰、陰卦、多陽、○其故、何也。陽卦、奇、陰卦、耦、○其德行、何也。陽、一君而二民、君子之道也、陰、二君而一民、小人之道也。(以上 第四章)

●易曰、憧憧往來、朋從爾思。子曰、天下何思何慮 天下同歸而殊塗、一致而百慮、天下何思何慮。○日往則月來、月往則日來、日月、相推而明生焉、寒往則暑來、暑往則寒來、寒暑相推而歲成焉。往者、屈也、來者、信也、屈信、相感而利生焉。

●尺蠖之屈、以求信也、龍蛇之蟄、以存身也。精義入神、以致用也、利用安身、以崇德也。○過此以往、未之或知也、窮神知化、德之盛也。

●易曰、困于石、據于蒺蔾、入于其宮、不見其妻、凶。子曰、非所困而困焉、名必辱、非所據而據焉、身必危。旣辱且危、死期將至、妻其可得見邪。○易曰、公用射隼于高墉之上、獲之、无不利。子曰、隼者、禽也、弓矢者、器也、射之者、人也。君子藏器于身、待時而動、何不利之有。動而不括、是以出而有獲、語成器而動者也。

해가 지면 달이 뜨고, 달이 지면 해가 뜨며, 해와 달이 서로 밀쳐서 밝음이 생기며, 추위가 가면 더위가 오고, 더위가 가면 추위가 오니, 추위와 더위가 서로 밀쳐서 한 해를 이룬다. 가는 것은 굽히는 것이요, 오는 것은 펴는 것이니, 굽히고 펴는 것이 서로 감응하여 이로움이 생긴다.
자벌레가 굽히는 것은 펴기를 구하는 것이요, 용과 뱀이 숨는 것은 몸을 보존하려는 것이요, 정미로운 의리로 입신하려는 것은 쓰려는 것이요, 이롭게 써서 몸을 편안히 하는 것은 덕을 숭상하는 것이다.

The sun goes and the moon comes; the moon goes and the sun comes;—the sun and moon thus take the place each of the other, and their shining is the result. The cold goes and the heat comes; the heat goes and the cold comes;—it is by this mutual succession of the cold and heat that the year is completed. That which goes becomes less and less, and that which comes waxes more and more;—it is by the influence on each other of this contraction and expansion that the advantages of the different conditions are produced.
When the looper coils itself up, it thereby straightens itself again; when worms and snakes go into the state of hybernation, they thereby keep themselves alive. So, when we minutely investigate the nature and reasons of things, till we have entered into the inscrutable and spirit-like in them, we attain to the largest practical application of them; when that application becomes the quickest and readiest, and all personal restfulness is secured, our virtue is thereby exalted.

이를 넘는 것은 알지 못하는 것이니, 신묘한 이치를 궁구해서 변화의 법칙을 아는 것은 덕의 왕성함이다.

역易에서 말하기를, 돌에 걸려 곤궁하며 가시덤불에 의지한다. 그 집에 들어가더라도 그 아내를 보지 못하여 흉하다 하니, 공자가 말씀하시길, 곤궁할 바가 아닌데 곤궁하니 이름이 반드시 더럽혀지고, 의지할 데가 아닌데 의지하니 몸이 위태로워진다. 이미 더럽혀지고 위태해서 죽을 시기가 장차 이르니, 아내를 볼 수 있을 것인가? 역易에 말하기를, 공公이 높은 담 위의 새매를 쏴서 잡으니, 이롭지 않음이 없다 하니, 공자가 말씀하시길, 준隼은 새요, 활과 화살은 기구요, 쏘는 것은 사람이니,

Going on beyond this, we reach a point which it is hardly possible to know. We have thoroughly comprehended the inscrutable and spirit-like, and know the processes of transformation; —this is the fulness of virtue.

It is said in the *Yi*, 'The third line shows its subject distressed before a rock, and trying to lay hold of thorns; entering into his palace and not seeing his wife: —there will be evil.' The Master said: —'If one be distressed by what need not distress him, his name is sure to be disgraced; if he lay hold on what he should not touch, his life is sure to be imperilled. In disgrace and danger, his death will soon come; —is it possible for him in such circumstances to see his wife?' It is said in the *Yi*, 'The duke with his bow shoots at the falcon on the top of the high wall; he hits it: —his every movement will be advantageous.' The Master said: —'The falcon is a bird of prey; the bow and arrow is a weapon of war; the shooter is a man.

군자가 기구를 몸에 간직했다가 때를 기다려 움직이면 어찌 이롭지 않음이 있을 것인가? 움직임에 막히지 않는 것이다. 이로써 나가서 잡을 수 있으니, 도구를 만든 뒤에 움직이는 것을 말한 것이다.
공자가 말씀하시길, 소인은 어질지 못함을 부끄러워하지 않으며, 의롭지 못함을 두려워하지 않는다. 이롭지 않으면 권하지 않으며, 위엄스럽지 않으면 무서워하지 않으니, 적게 징계하여 크게 경계함이 소인의 복이다. 역易에서 말하기를, 형틀을 신겨서 발꿈치를 없애어 허물이 없다 하니, 이것을 말한 것이다.

The superior man keeps his weapon concealed about his person, and waits for the proper time to move; —doing this, how should his movement be other than successful? There is nothing to fetter or embarrass his movement; and hence, when he comes forth, he succeeds in his object. The language speaks of movement when the instrument necessary to it is ready and perfect.'
The Master said: —'The small man is not ashamed of what is not benevolent, nor does he fear to do what is not righteous. Without the prospect of gain he does not stimulate himself to what is good, nor does he correct himself without being moved. Self-correction, however, in what is small will make him careful in what would be of greater consequence; —and this is the happiness of the small man. It is said in the *Yi*, "His feet are in the stocks, and he is disabled in his toes: —there will be no further occasion for blame."'

●子曰、小人、不恥不仁、不畏不義、不見利、不勸、不威、不懲。小懲而大誠此小人之福也。易曰屨校滅趾、无咎、此之謂也。○善不積、不足以成名、惡不積、不足以滅身。小人、以小善、爲无益而弗爲也、以小惡、爲无傷而弗去也、故、惡積而不可掩、罪大而不可解。易曰、何校、滅耳、凶。

●子曰、危者、安其位者也、亡者、保其存者也、亂者、有其治者也。是故、君子安而不忘危、存而不忘亡、治而不忘亂。是以身安而國家、可保也。易曰其亡其亡、繫于苞桑。○子曰、德薄而位尊、知小而謀大、力小而任重、鮮不及矣。易曰、鼎、折足、覆公餗、其形、渥、凶。言不勝其任也。

●子曰、知幾其神乎。君子上交不諂、下交不瀆、其知幾乎。幾者、動之微、吉之先見者也。君子見幾而作、不俟終日。易曰、介于石、不終日、貞、吉。介如石焉、寧用終日。斷可識矣。君子知微知彰知柔知剛、萬夫之望。○子曰、顏氏之子、其殆庶幾乎。有不善、未嘗不知、知之、未嘗復行也。易曰、不遠復、无祇悔、元吉。

선을 쌓지 않으면 아름다운 이름을 이룰 수 없고, 악을 쌓지 않으면 몸을 해치지 않으니, 소인은 조금 착한 것을 이익될 것이 없다고 하여 하지 않으며, 조금 악한 것을 상함이 없다 하여 버리지 않는다. 그러므로 악을 쌓아서 가리지 않으며, 죄가 커져서 풀지 못한다. 역易에 말하기를, 형틀을 메서 귀를 없앤다고 하니 흉하다고 하였다.

공자가 말씀하시길, 위태롭게 여기는 것은 그 자리를 편안하게 할 것이요, 망할까 염려하는 것은 존재를 보존할 것이요, 어지러울까 여기는 것은 그 다스림이 있는 것이니, 이런 까닭에 군자는 편안해도 위태로움을 잊지 않으며, 있어도 없어짐을 잊지 않으며,

If acts of goodness be not accumulated, they are not sufficient to give its finish to one's name; if acts of evil be not accumulated, they are not sufficient to destroy one's life. The small man thinks that small acts of goodness are of no benefit, and does not do them; and that small deeds of evil do no harm, and does not abstain from them. Hence his wickedness becomes great till it cannot be covered, and his guilt becomes great till cannot be pardoned. This is what the *Yi* says, 'He wears the cangue and his ears are destroyed:—there will be evil.'

The Master said:—'He who keeps danger in mind is he who will rest safe in his seat; he who keeps ruin in mind is he who will preserve his interests secure; he who sets the danger of disorder before him is he who will maintain the state of order. Therefore the superior man, when resting in safety, does not forget that danger may come; when in a state of security, he does not forget the possibility of ruin;

다스려도 어지러움을 잊지 않는다. 이로써 몸이 편안하고 나라를 보존할 수 있다. 역易에서 말하기를, 그 망할까 망할까 염려해야 더부룩한 뽕나무가 맨다고 한다. 공자가 말씀하시기를, 덕이 박한데 자리는 높으며, 지혜는 작은데 도모하는 일은 크며, 힘은 적은데 책임이 무거우면, 재앙이 미치지 않는 이가 적다고 하였다. 역易에 말하기를 솥의 발이 부러져 공의 밥을 엎으니, 그 형체가 젖어 흉하다 하니, 이는 그 책임을 이기지 못함을 말한 것이다.
공자가 말씀하시길, 기미를 아는 것이 신일진저! 군자는 윗사람을 사귐에 아첨하지 않으며, 아랫사람을 사귐에 함부로 하지 않으니, 그 기미를 아는 것일진저!

and when all is in a state of order, he does not forget that disorder may come. Thus his person is kept safe, and his states and all their clans can be preserved. This is according to what the *Yi* says, "Let him say, 'Shall I perish? shall I perish?' so shall this state be firm, as if bound to a clump of bushy mulberry trees.'" The Master said:—'Virtue small and office high; wisdom small and plans great; strength small and burden heavy:—where such conditions exist, it is seldom that they do not end in evil. As is said in the *Yi*, "The tripod's feet are overthrown, and the ruler's food is overturned. The body of him who is thus indicated is wet with shame:—there will be evil."'
The Master said:—'Does not he who knows the springs of things possess spirit-like wisdom? The superior man, in his intercourse with the high, uses no flattery, and, in his intercourse with the low, no coarse freedom:—does not this show that he knows the springs of things?

기미는 움직임이 은밀한 것이니 길함이 먼저 나타나는 것이다. 군자는 기미를 보고 일어나서 종일을 기다리지 않으니, 역易에서 말하기를, 절개節介가 돌이라 하루를 마치지 않아서 바르고 길하다 하니, 절개가 돌과 같으니 어찌 날을 마치도록 기다리겠는가? 판단하여 아는 것이다. 군자가 기미를 알고 드러난 것도 알며 부드러움도 알고 강함도 아니, 수많은 사람이 우러러 본다. 공자가 말씀하시길, 안씨顔氏의 아들(顔子)이 도道에 가까울진저! 착하지 않음이 있으면 일찍이 알지 못함이 없으며, 알면 다시 행하지 않는다. 역易에서 말하기를, 멀지 않아 회복하여 후회하는데 이르지 않으니, 크게 길한 것이다.

Those springs are the slight beginnings of movement, and the earliest indications of good fortune or ill. The superior man sees them, and acts accordingly without waiting for the delay of a single day. As is said in the *Yi*, "He is firm as a rock, and acts without the delay of a single day. With firm goodness there will be good fortune." Firm as a rock, how should he have to wait a single day to ensure his knowing those springs and his course? The superior man knows the minute and the manifested; he knows what is week, and what is strong:—he is a model to ten thousand.' The Master said:—'I may venture to say that the son of the Yan family had nearly attained the standard of perfection. If anything that he did was not good, he was sure to become conscious of that; and when he knew it, he did not do the thing again. As is said in the *Yi*, "The first line shows its subject returning from an error that has not led him far away. There is no occasion for repentance. There will be great good."

●天地絪縕、萬物、化醇、男女構精、萬物化生。易曰、三人行、則損一人、一人行、則得其友、言致一也。○子曰、君子安其身而後、動、易其心而後、語、定其交而後、求、君子脩此三者故、全也。危以動、則民不與也、懼以語、則民不應也、无交而求、則民不與也、莫之與、則傷之者至矣。易曰、莫益之、或擊之、立心勿恒、凶。(以上 第五章)

●子曰、乾坤、其易之門邪。乾、陽物也、坤、陰物也。陰陽、合德、而剛柔有體、以體天地之撰、以通神明之德。○其稱名也、雜而不越、於稽其類、其衰世之意耶。

●夫易、彰往而察來、而微顯闡幽。開而當名、辨物、正言、斷辭、則備矣。

●其稱名也小、其取類也大、其旨遠、其辭文、其言、曲而中、其事肆而隱。因貳、以濟民行、以明失得之報。(以上 第六章)

●易之興也、其於中古乎。作易者、其有憂患乎。○是故、履、德之基也、謙、德之柄也、復、德之本也、恒、德之固也、損、德之修也、益、德之裕也、困、德之辨也、井、德之地也、巽、德之制也。

천지의 기운이 뭉치니 만물이 변화하여 숙성해지고, 남녀가 정기를 얽히니 만물이 변화하여 생성된다 역易에서 말하기를, 세 사람이 가는 데는 한 사람을 덜고, 한 사람이 가면 그 벗을 얻는다 하니, 하나를 이룸을 말한 것이다. 공자가 말씀하시길, 군자는 그 몸을 편안히 한 뒤에야 움직이며, 그 마음을 평안하게 한 뒤에야 말하며, 그 사귐을 정한 뒤에야 구하니, 군자가 이 세가지를 닦았기에 온전하다. 위태롭게 움직이면 곧 백성이 참여하지 아니하고, 두려워하면서 말하면 곧 백성이 응하지 아니하며, 사귐이 없이 구하면 곧 백성이 함께 하지 아니 하고,

There is an intermingling of the genial influences of heaven and earth, and transformation in its various forms abundantly proceeds. There is an intercommunication of seed between male and female, and transformation in its living types proceeds. What is said in the *Yi*, 'Three individuals are walking together and one is made to disappear; there is but one man walking, and he gets his mate,' tells us of the effort in nature at oneness of operation. The Master said:—'The superior man in a high place composes himself before he tries to move others; makes his mind restful and easy before he speaks; settles the principles of his intercourse with others before he seeks anything from them. The superior man cultivates these three things, and so is complete. If he try to move others while he is himself in unrest, the people will not act with him; if he speak while he is himself in a state of apprehension, the people will not respond to him; if without certain principles of intercommunication, he issue his requests, the people will not grant them.

함께 하지 아니하면 곧 해치는 자가 이르게 된다. 역易에서 말하기를, 더하지 말라 또는 칠 것이니, 마음을 가짐이 일정치 못함이 흉하다고 하였다.
공자가 말씀하시길, 건乾과 곤坤은 그 역易의 문門이다. 건은 양물陽物이요, 곤은 음물陰物이니, 음과 양은 덕을 합해서 강剛과 유柔의 몸체가 있다. 이로써 천지의 일을 본받고 신명의 덕을 통한다. 그 일컬어지는 이름이 잡다해도 넘지 않으나, 그 종류를 고찰해보면 쇠미한 세상의 뜻일진저.

When there are none to accord with him, those who work to injure him will make their appearance. As is said in the *Yi*, " We see one to whose advantage none will contribute, while some will seek to assail him. He observes no regular rule in the ordering of his heart:— there will be evil." '
The Master said:—'The trigrams *Qian* and *Kun* may be regarded as the gate of the *Yi*.' *Qian* represents what is of the *yang* nature bright and active; *Kun* what is of the *yin* nature shaded and inactive. These two unite according to their qualities, and there comes the embodiment of the result by the strong and weak lines. In this way we have the phenomena of heaven and earth visibly exhibited, and can comprehend the operation of the spiritual intelligence. The appellations and names of the diagrams and lines are various, but do not go beyond what is to be ascribed to the operation of these two conditions. When we examine the nature and style of the appended explanations, they seem to express the ideas of a decaying age.

대저 역易은 지난 것을 드러내고 오는 것을 살피며, 은밀한 것을 드러내고 그윽한 것을 밝히며, 괘효卦爻를 열어서 이름에 맞게 하며, 사물을 분별하여 말을 바르게 하니, 말로 판단하면 곧 갖추어질 것이다. 그 일컫는 명칭은 작지만 취하는 종류는 크며, 그 뜻은 원대하고 그 말은 아름다우며, 그 말이 간곡하고 꼭 맞으며, 그 일은 펴놓되 이치는 은밀하다. 두가지로 인해 백성의 행동을 제도하여 득실의 결과를 밝혀야 할 것이다.
역易의 일어난 때는 그 중고中古인가! 역易을 지은 자는 근심과 걱정이 있었던 것인가?

The *Yi* exhibits the past, and teaches us to discriminate the issues of the future; it makes manifest what is minute, and brings to light what is obscure. Then king Wan opened its symbols, and distinguished things in accordance with its names, so that all his words were correct and his explanations decisive;—the book was now complete. The appellations and names of the diagrams and lines are but small matters, but the classes of things comprehended under them are large. Their scope reaches far, and the explanations attached to them are elegant. The words are indirect, but to the point; the matters seem plainly set forth, but there is a secret principle in them. Their object is, in cases that are doubtful, to help the people in their conduct, and to make plain the recompenses of good and evil.
Was it not in the middle period of antiquity that the *Yi* began to flourish? Was not he who made it familiar with anxiety and calamity?

●履、和而至、謙、尊而光、復、小而辨於物、恒、雜而不厭、損、先難而後易、益、長裕而不設、困、窮而通、井、居其所而遷、巽、稱而隱。○履以和行、謙以制禮、復以自知、恒以一德、損以遠害、益以興利、困以寡怨、井以辯義、巽以行權。(以上 第七章)

●易之爲書也、不可遠。爲道也屢遷、變動不居、周流六虛、上下无常、剛柔相易、不可爲曲要、唯變所適、○其出入以度、外內、使知懼、○又明於憂患與故。无有師保、如臨父母、○初率其辭而揆其方、旣有曲常。苟非其人、道不虛行。(以上 第八章)

●易之爲書也、原始要終、以爲質也。六爻相雜、唯其時物也。○其初、難知、其上、易知、本末也。初辭擬之、卒成之終。○若夫雜物、撰德、辯是與非、則非其中爻、不備。○噫、亦要存亡吉凶、則居可知矣。知者觀其彖辭、則思過半矣。

●二與四同功而異位、其善、不同、二多譽、四多懼、近也。柔之爲道不利遠者、其要无咎、其用柔中也、○三與五同功而異位、三多凶、五多功、貴賤之等也。其柔危、其剛勝耶。(以上 第九章)

이런 까닭에 이괘履卦는 덕의 기초이고, 겸謙은 덕의 자루이며, 복復은 덕의 근본이고, 항恒은 덕의 굳음이며, 손損은 덕의 닦음이고, 익益은 덕의 넉넉함이며, 곤困은 덕의 분별함이고, 정井은 덕의 터전이며, 손巽은 덕의 제도制度이다.
이履는 조화로우면서 이르고, 겸謙은 높으면서 빛나고, 복復은 작으면서 사물을 분별하고, 항恒은 섞여도 싫어하지 아니하고, 손損은 먼저는 어렵지만 나중은 쉽고, 익益은 넉넉히 길러주되 베풀지 않으며, 곤困은 궁하되 통하고, 정井은 제자리에 있되 옮겨지고, 손巽은 저울질하되 은밀하다.

Therefore the 10th diagram, *Lu*, shows us the foundation of virtue; the 15th, *Qian*, its handle; the 24th, *Fu*, its root; the 32nd, *Heng*, its solidity; the 41st, *Sun*, its cultivation; the 42nd, *Yi*, its abundance; the 47th, *Kun*, its exercise of discrimination; the 48th, *Jing*, its field; and the 57th, *Xun*, its regulation.
In *Lu* we have the perfection of harmony; in *Qian*, we have the giving honour to others, and the distinction thence arising; in *Fu* we have what is small at first, but there is in it a nice discrimination of the qualities of things; in *Heng* we have a mixed experience, but without any weariness; in *Xun* we have difficulty in the beginning and ease in the end; in *Yi* we have abundance of growth without any contrivance; in *Kun* we have the pressure of extreme difficulty, ending in a free course; in *Jing* we have abiding in one's place and at the same time removal to meet the movement of others; and in *Xun* we have the weighing of things and action accordingly, but secretly and unobserved.

이履로써 행동을 조화롭게 하고, 겸謙으로써 예를 만들며, 복復으로써 자신을 알고, 항恒으로써 덕을 한결같이 하며, 손損으로서 해害를 멀리하고, 익益으로서 이익을 일으키며, 곤困으로써 원망을 적게 하고, 정井으로서 의義를 분별하며, 손巽으로써 권權을 행한다.
역易의 글은 멀리할 수 없는 것이요, 도道는 자주 바뀌는 것이니, 변동해서 한 곳에 있지 않고, 여섯자리에 두루 흘러서 오르고 내림에 일정함이 없으며, 강剛과 유柔가 서로 바뀌어 일정한 방식이 되지 못하고 오직 가는대로 변하니, 나가고 들어가는데 법도로서 삼으며,

The use of *Lu* appears in the harmony of the conduct; of *Qian*, in the regulation of ceremonies; of *Fu*, in self-knowledge; of *Heng*, in uniformity of virtue; of *Xun*, in keeping what is harmful at a distance; of *Yi*, in the promotion of what is advantageous; of *Kun*, in the diminution of resentments; of *Jing*, in the discrimination of what is righteous; and of *Xun*, in the doing of what is appropriate to time and to circumstances.
The *Yi* is a book which should not be let slip from the mind. Its method of teaching is marked by the frequent changing of its lines. They change and move without staying in one place, flowing about into any one of the six places of the hexagram. They ascend and descend, ever inconstant. The strong and the weak lines change places, so that an invariable and compendious rule cannot be derived from them;—it must vary as their changes indicate. The goings forth and comings in of the lines are according to rule and measure.

밖과 안에 두려운 것을 알게 하며, 또 우환과 그 연고에 밝다. 스승은 없으나 부모가 와 있는 것 같으니, 처음에 그 괘효사에 따라 그 방법을 헤아려보면, 이미 일정한 법도가 있다. 진실로 그 사람이 아니면 도가 헛되이 행해지지 않을 것이다.
역易의 글은 시작을 살피고 마침을 요약하여 바탕으로 삼는다. 육효六爻가 서로 섞이는 것은 오직 그 때의 사물이다. 그 처음(초효)은 알기 어렵고 그 위(상효)는 알기 쉬우니, 본本과 말末이다. 처음의 말은 비기고 끝에서는 이루어서 마칠 것이다.

People learn from them in external and internal affairs to stand in awe. The book, moreover, makes plain the nature of anxieties and calamities, and the causes of them. Though its students have neither master nor guardian, it is as if their parents drew near to them. Beginning with taking note of its explanations, we reason out the principles to which they point. We thus find out that it does supply a constant and standard rule. But if there be not the proper men to carry this out, the course cannot be pursued without them.
The *Yi* is a book in which the form of each diagram is determined by the lines from the first to the last, which must be carefully observed. The six lines are mixed together, according to the time when they enter the figure and their substance as whole and divided. There is difficulty in knowing the significance of the first line, while to know that of the topmost line is easy; —they form the beginning and the end of the diagram. The explanation of the first line tasks the calculating of the makers, but in the end they had but to complete this.

대저 사물이 섞인 것에서 덕을 가리는 것과 시비를 분별하는 것은 중효中爻가 아니면 갖추지 못할 것이다. 아아! 또한 존망과 길흉을 알려고 한다면 가만히 있어도 알 수 있다. 지혜로운 자는 그 단사彖辭를 보면 생각이 반을 넘을 것이다.
이효二爻와 사효四爻는 공은 같아도 자리는 달라서 그 착함이 같지 않으니, 이효에는 명예가 많고 사효에는 두려움이 많은 것은 가깝기 때문이다. 유柔의 도道는 먼 것이 이롭지 않지만, 그 허물이 없는 것은 그 유柔로 중中을 쓰기 때문이다.

As to the variously-disposed intermediate lines with their diverse formations, for determining their qualities, and discriminating the right and wrong in them, we should be unprovided but for the explanations of them. Yea, moreover, if we wish to know what is likely to be preserved and what to perish, what will be lucky and what will be unlucky, this may easily be known from the explanations of the different lines. But if the wise will look at the explanations of the entire diagrams, their thoughts will embrace more than half of this knowledge.
The second and fourth lines are of the same quality as being in even places, but their positions with respect to the fifth line are different, and their value is not the same; but the second is the object of much commendation, and the fourth the subject of many apprehensions,—from its nearness to that line. But for a line in a place of weakness it is not good to be far from the occupant of the place of strength, and what its subject should desire in such a case is merely to be without blame. The advantage here is in the second line being in the central place.

삼효三爻와 오효五爻가 공功이 같아도 자리는 달라서, 삼효에 흉이 많고 오효에 공功이 많은 것은, 귀천이 차등이 있기 때문이다. 그 유柔는 위태하고 그 강剛은 이길 것이다.
역易의 글은 넓고 크게 다 갖추어서 천도天道가 있고, 인도人道가 있으며, 지도地道가 있으니, 삼재를 겸해서 둘로 나눈다. 그러므로 여섯이니. 여섯이란 다른 것이 아니라 삼재의 도이다. 도에는 변동이 있으므로 효爻를 말하고, 효에 차등이 있으므로 사물이라 말하며, 사물이 서로 섞여 있으므로 문文이라고 말한다.

The third and fifth lines are of the same quality, as being in odd places, but their positions are different; and the occupant of the third meets with many misfortunes, while the occupant of the fifth achieves much merit:—this arises from one being in the noble position and the other in the mean. Are they occupied by the symbol of weakness? There will be peril. By that of strength? There will be victory.
The *Yi* is a book of wide comprehension and great scope, embracing everything. There are in it the way of heaven, the way of man, and the way of earth. It then takes the lines representing those three Powers, and doubles them till they amount to six. What these six lines show is simply this,—the way of the three Powers. This way is marked by changes and movements, and hence we have the imitative lines. Those lines are of different grades in the trigrams, and hence we designate them from their component elements. These are mixed together, and elegant forms arise.

●易之爲書也、廣大悉備、有天道焉、有人道焉、有地道焉、兼三材而兩之。故、六、六者、非他也、三才之道也。○道有變動、故曰爻、爻有等、故曰物、物相雜、故曰文。文不當、故、吉凶、生焉。(以上 第十章)

●易之興也、其當殷之末世周之盛德耶、當文王與紂之事邪。是故、其辭危、危者、使平、易者、使傾、其道甚大、百物、不廢、懼以終始、其要无咎、此之謂易之道也。(以上 第十一章)

●夫乾、天下之至健也、德行、恒易以知險、夫坤、天下之至順也、德行、恒簡以知阻。○能說諸心、能研諸侯之慮、定天下之吉凶、成天下之亹亹者。

●是故、變化云爲、吉事、有祥。象事、知器、占事、知來。○天地設位、聖人、成能、人謀鬼謀、百姓、與能。

●八卦、以象告、爻彖、以情言、剛柔雜居而吉凶、可見矣。○變動、以利言、吉凶、以情遷。是故、愛惡相攻而吉凶、生、遠近、相取而悔吝、生、情僞、相感而利害生。凡易之情、近而不相得、則凶或害之、悔且吝。

●將叛者其辭慙、中心疑者、其辭枝、吉人之辭、寡、躁人之辭、多、誣善之人、其辭游、失其守者、其辭屈。(以上 第十二章)

문文은 합당치 않으므로 길흉이 생겨난다.
역易이 일어난 것은 은殷나라의 말세와 주周나라의 덕이 왕성할 무렵이며, 문왕文王과 주왕紂王의 일에 해당할 것이다. 이런 까닭에 그 말이 위태하여, 위태로운 자를 태평하게 하고 소홀히 하는 자는 쓰러뜨리니, 그 도道는 심히 커서 온갖 사물을 폐廢하지 않으나, 이로써 처음부터 끝까지 두려워하면 반드시 허물이 없을 것이니, 이것을 일러 역易의 도라고 한다.
대저 건乾은 천하의 지극히 강건한 것이니, 덕행이 항상 쉬우면서 위험한 것을 알며,

When such forms are not in their appropriate places, the ideas of good fortune and bad are thus produced.
Was it not in the last age of *Yan*, when the virtue of *Zhou* had reached its highest point, and during the troubles between king Wen and the tyrant *Zhou*, that the study of the *Yi* began to flourish? On this account the explanations in the book express a feeling of anxious apprehension, and teach how peril may be turned into security, and easy carelessness is sure to meet with overthrow. The method in which these things come about is very comprehensive, and must be acknowledged in every sphere of things. If at the beginning there be a cautious apprehension as to the end, there will probably be no error or cause for blame. This is what is called the way of the *Yi*.
The hexagram *Qian* represents the strongest of all under the sky. Through this quality its operations are always manifested with ease, for it knows where there would be peril and embarrassment.

곤坤은 천하의 지극히 유순한 것니, 덕행이 항상 간략하면서 막힌 것을 안다. 능히 마음에 기쁘게 하며 능히 제후의 생각을 연구하여, 천하의 길흉을 정하고 천하가 힘쓰는 것을 완성하도록 한다. 이런 까닭에 변화를 일러 말함에 길한 일에는 상서로운 조짐이 있다. 일을 본받아 기물을 알며, 일을 점쳐서 미래를 안다. 천지가 자리를 베품에 성인聖人이 능력을 이루니, 사람이 꾀하고 귀신이 꾀함에 백성이 그 능력있는 이와 함께 한다.

The hexagram *Kun* represents the most docile of all under the sky. Through this quality its operations are always manifested with the promptest decision, for it knows where there would be obstruction. The sages, who are thus represented, and who made the *Yi*, were able to rejoice in heart in the absolute truth of things, and were able also to weigh carefully all matters that could occasion anxiety; thus they fixed the good and bad fortune of all things under the sky, and could accomplish the things requiring strenuous efforts. Therefore amid the changes and transformations taking place in heaven and earth, and the words and deeds of men, events that are to be fortunate have their happy omens. The sages knew the definite principles underlying the prognostications of the former class, and the future of those of the latter, now to be ascertained by divination. The places of heaven and earth in the diagrams having been determined, the sages were able by means of the *Yi* to carry out and complete their ability. In this way even the common people were able to share with them in deciding about the counsels of men and the counsels of spiritual beings.

팔괘八卦는 상象으로써 고하고, 효사爻辭와 단사彖辭는 정情으로써 말하니, 강剛과 유柔는 뒤섞여 있어 길과 흉을 볼 수 있다. 변동은 이로움으로써 말하고 길흉은 정으로써 옮긴다. 이런 까닭에 사랑과 미움이 서로 부딪쳐서 길과 흉이 생기고, 먼 것과 가까운 것이 서로를 취함에 회린悔吝이 생기며, 진정과 거짓이 서로 감응하여 이로움과 해로움이 생기니, 역易의 정情이 가까워도 서로 어울리지 못하면, 흉하거나 해로워서 후회하고 또 궁색하게 될 것이다.

The eight trigrams communicate their information by their emblematic figures. The explanations appended to the lines and the completed figures tell how the contemplation of them affected the makers. The strong and the weak lines appear mixed in them, and thus the good and the evil which they indicate can be seen. The changes and movements which take place in the manipulation of the stalks and the formation of the diagrams speak as from the standpoint of what is advantageous. The intimations of good and evil vary according to the place and nature of the lines. Thus they may indicate a mutual influence in any two of them of love or hatred, and good or evil is the result; or that mutual influence may be affected by the nearness of the lines to, or their distance from, each other, and then repentance or regret is the result; or the influence may be that of truth or of hypocrisy, and then the result is what is advantageous, or what is injurious. In all these relations of the lines in the *Yi* if two are near and do not blend harmoniously, there may be all these results,—evil, or what is injurious, or occasion for repentance and regret.

장차 배반하려는 자는 그 말에 부끄러워하는 기색이 있고, 마음 속으로 의심하는 자는 그 말이 이리저리 갈라지며, 길한 사람의 말은 적고, 조급한 사람의 말은 많으며, 선을 속이는 사람은 그 말이 놀고, 그 지킬 것(지조)을 잃은 사람은 그 말이 비굴하다.

The language of him who is meditating a revolt from the right betrays his inward shame; that of him whose inward heart doubts about it diverges to other topics. The words of a good man are few; those of a coarse man are many. The words of one who slanders what is good are unsubstantial; those of him who is losing what he ought to keep are crooked.

● 昔者聖人之作易也、幽贊於神明而生蓍、○參天兩地而倚數、○觀變於陰陽而立卦、發揮於剛柔而生爻、○和順於道德而理於義、窮理盡性、以至於命。（以上 第一章）

● 昔者聖人之作易也、將以順性命之理、是以立天之道曰陰與陽、立地之道曰柔與剛、立人之道曰仁與義。兼三才而兩之、故易六畫而成卦、分陰分陽、迭用柔剛、故、易、六位而成章。（以上 第二章）

● 天地定位、山澤、通氣、雷風、相薄、水火不相射、八卦相錯、○數往者、順、知來者、逆、是故、易、逆數也。（以上 第三章）

● 雷以動之、風以散之、雨以潤之、日以烜之、艮以止之、兌以說之、乾以君之、坤以藏之。（以上 第四章）

● 帝、出乎震、齊乎巽、相見乎離、致役乎坤、說言乎兌、戰乎乾、勞乎坎、成言乎艮。

옛날 성인이 역易을 지을 때, 신명神明을 그윽히 도와서 시초蓍草를 내었고, 하늘은 셋으로, 땅을 둘로 하여 수數를 정했으며, 음양陰陽의 변화를 관찰하여 괘卦를 세우고, 강유剛柔의 변화를 발휘하여 효爻를 내었으니, 도덕道德에 화순和順하고 의로움을 따르며, 이치를 궁구하고 본성을 다하여 명命에 이르렀다.
옛날 성인이 역易을 지을 때, 장차 성명性命의 이치에 순응하려 하였으니,

Anciently, when the sages made the *Yi*, in order to give mysterious assistance to the spiritual Intelligences, they produced the rules for the use of the divining plant. The number 3 was assigned to heaven, 2 to earth, and from these came the other numbers. They contemplated the changes in the divided and undivided lines by the process of manipulating the stalks, and formed the trigrams; from the movements that took place in the strong and weak lines, they produced their teaching about the separate lines. There ensued a harmonious conformity to the course of duty and to virtue, with a discrimination of what was right in each particular case. They thus made an exhaustive discrimination of what was right, and effected the complete development of every nature, till they arrived in the *Yi* at what was appointed for it by Heaven.
Anciently, when the sages made the *Yi*, it was with the design that its figures should be in conformity with the principles underlying the natures of men and things, and the ordinances for them appointed by Heaven.

이로써 하늘의 도를 세워서 음陰과 양陽이라 하고, 땅의 도를 세워서 유柔와 강剛이라고 하며, 사람의 도를 세워서 인仁과 의義라고 하였다. 삼재三才를 겸하여 둘로 구분하니, 그러므로 역易이 육획六畫으로 괘를 이루고, 음陰과 양陽을 나누며, 유柔와 강剛을 번갈아 사용하니, 그러므로 역易은 여섯자리로 드러나 장을 이루게 되었다.
천지가 자리를 정하고 산과 못이 기운을 통하며, 우뢰와 바람이 서로 부딪치고, 물과 불이 서로 치지 않아서, 팔괘八卦가 서로 섞이니, 지나간 것을 헤아려 보는 것은 순하고, 오는 것을 아는 것은 거슬리는 것이니, 이런 까닭에 역易은 거슬러 셈하는 것이다.

With this view they exhibited in them the way of heaven, calling the lines *yin* and *yang*; the way of earth, calling them the weak or soft and the strong or hard; and the way of men, under the names of benevolence and righteousness. Each trigram embraced those three Powers; and, being repeated, its full form consisted of six lines. A distinction was made of the places assigned to the *yin* and *yang* lines, which were variously occupied, now by the strong and now by the weak forms, and thus the figure of each hexagram was completed.
The symbols of heaven and earth received their determinate positions; those for mountains and collections of water interchanged their influences; those for thunder and wind excited each other the more; and those for water and fire did each other no harm. Then among these eight symbols there was a mutual communication. The numbering of the past is a natural process; the knowledge of the coming is anticipation. Therefore in the *Yi* we have both anticipation and the natural process.

우뢰로써 움직이고 바람으로써 흩어지며, 비로써 적시고 해로써 말리며, 산에 그치고 못에 기뻐하며, 건乾은 임금이 되고, 곤坤은 품는다.
제帝는 진震에서 나서 손巽에서 가지런해지며, 이離에서 서로 보고, 곤坤에서 역사役事를 이루며, 태兌에서 말을 기뻐하고 건乾에서 싸우며, 감坎에서 위로하고, 간艮에서 말을 이룬다.
만물이 진震에서 나오니 진震은 동방이고, 손巽에서 가지런히 하니 손巽은 동남東南이며, 제齊라는 것은 만물이 깨끗하게 가지런히 하는 것을 말한다. 이離는 밝은 것이니,

Thunder serves to put things in motion; wind to scatter the genial seeds of them; rain to moisten them; the sun to warm them; what is symbolised by *Gen*, to arrest and keep them in their places; by *Dui*, to give them joyful course; by *Qian*, to rule them; and by *Kun*, to store them up.
God comes forth in *Zhen* to His producing work; He brings His processes into full and equal action in *Xun*; they are manifested to one another in *Li*; the greatest service is done for Him in *Kun*; He rejoices in *Dui*; He struggles in *Qian*; He is comforted and enters into rest in *Kan*; and He completes the work of the year in *Gen*.
All things are made to issue forth in *Zhen*, which is placed at the east. The processes of production are brought into full and equal action in *Xun*, which is placed at the south-east. The being brought into full and equal action refers to the purity and equal arrangement of all things. *Li* gives the idea of brightness.

● 萬物出乎震、震東方也、齊乎巽、巽、東南也、齊也者、言萬物之絜齊也。離也者、明也、萬物皆相見、南方之卦也。聖人、南面而聽天下、嚮明而治、蓋取諸此也。坤也者、地也、萬物、皆致養焉、故、曰致役乎坤。

● 兌、正秋也、萬物之所說也、故、曰說言乎兌。戰乎乾、乾、西北之卦也、言陰陽相薄也。坎者、水也、正北方之卦也、勞卦也、萬物之所歸也、故、曰勞乎坎。艮、東北之卦也、萬物之所成終而所成始也、故、曰成言乎艮。（以上 第五章）

● 神也者、妙萬物而爲言者也。動萬物者莫疾乎雷、橈萬物者莫疾乎風、燥萬物者莫熯乎火、說萬物者莫說乎澤、潤萬物者莫潤乎水、終萬物始萬物者莫盛乎艮。故、水火相逮、雷風、不相悖、山澤、通氣然後、能變化、旣成萬物也。（以上 第六章）

● 乾、健也、坤、順也、震、動也、巽、入也、坎、陷也、離、麗也、艮、止也、兌、說也。（以上 第七章）

만물이 다 서로 보게 되니 남방南方의 괘卦이다. 성인이 남쪽을 향하여 천하의 의견을 들어서 천하를 밝게 다스리니, 대개 여기서 취한 것이다. 곤坤은 땅이니 만물이 모두 여기서 길러진다. 그러므로 곤坤에서 노역을 이룬다고 말한다.
태兌는 바로 가을로서 만물이 기뻐하는 것이니, 태兌에서 기뻐한다고 말한다. 건乾에서 싸운다는 것은 건乾은 서북西北의 괘卦이니, 음陰과 양陽이 서로 부딪치는 것을 말한다. 감坎은 물이니, 정북방正北方의 괘卦로서, 수고로운 괘이나 만물이 돌아가는 곳이니, 그러므로 감坎에서 위로한다고 말한다.

All things are now made manifest to one another. It is the trigram of the south. The sages turn their faces to the south when they give audience to all under the sky, administering government towards the region of brightness:—the idea in this procedure was taken from this. *Kun* denotes the earth, and is placed at the south-west. All things receive from it their fullest nourishment, and hence it is said, 'The greatest service is done for Him in *Kun*.'
Dui corresponds to the west and to the autumn,—the season in which all things rejoice. Hence it is said, 'He rejoices in *Dui*.' He struggles in *Qian*, which is the trigram of the north-west. The idea is that there the inactive and active conditions beat against each other. *Kan* denotes water. It is the trigram of the exact north,—the trigram of comfort and rest, what all things are tending to. Hence it is said, 'He is comforted and enters into rest in *Kan*.

간艮은 동북東北의 괘卦이니, 만물이 마침을 이루고, 비롯함을 이루는 것이니, 그러므로 간艮에서 이룬다고 말한다.
신神이란 만물을 오묘하게 함을 말한 것이니, 만물을 움직이는 것은 우뢰만큼 빠른 것이 없고, 만물을 흔드는 것은 바람보다 빠른 것이 없으며, 만물을 건조시키는 것은 불만한 것이 없고, 만물을 기쁘게 하는 것은 못만한 것이 없으며, 만물을 적시는 것은 물만한 것이 없고, 만물을 끝맺고 만물을 시작하는 것은 간艮만큼 왕성한 것이 없다. 그러므로 수화水火가 서로를 따르고, 우뢰와 바람이 서로 거스르지 않으며, 산과 못이 기운을 통하니, 그런 뒤에야 변화하여 만물을 이룬다.

In it all things bring to a full end the issues of the past year, and prepare the commencement of the next. Hence it is said, 'He completes the work of the year in *Gen*.'
When we speak of Spirit we mean the subtle presence and operation of God with all things. For putting all things in motion there is nothing more vehement than thunder; for scattering them there is nothing more effective than wind; for drying them up there is nothing more parching than fire; for giving them pleasure and satisfaction there is nothing more grateful than a lake or marsh; for moistening them there is nothing more enriching than water; for bringing them to an end and making them begin again there is nothing more fully adapted than *Gen*. Thus water and fire contribute together to the one object; thunder and wind do not act contrary to each other; mountains and collections of water interchange their influences. It is in this way, that they are able to change and transform, and to give completion to all things.

건乾은 강건健壯하고 곤坤은 손순하며, 진震은 움직이고 손巽은 들어가며, 감坎은 빠지고 이離는 걸리며, 간艮은 그치고, 태兌는 기뻐한다. 건乾은 말이 되고, 곤坤은 소가 되며, 진震은 용이 되고, 손巽은 닭이 되며, 감坎은 돼지가 되고, 이離는 꿩이 되며, 간艮은 개가 되고, 태兌는 양이 된다.

건乾은 머리고, 곤坤은 배며, 진震은 발이고, 손巽은 넓적다리이며, 감坎은 귀이고, 이離는 눈이며, 감艮은 손이고, 태兌는 입이다.

건乾은 하늘이니, 그러므로 아버지라 일컫고, 곤坤은 땅이니, 그러므로 어머니라 일컬으며, 진震은 첫번째 구하여 아들을 얻은 것이니, 장남長男이라 말하고,

Qian is the symbol of strength; *Kun*, of docility; *Zhen*, of stimulus to movement; *Xun*, of penetration; *Kan*, of what is precipitous and perilous; *Li*, of what is bright and what is catching; *Gen*, of stoppage or arrest; and *Dui*, of pleasure and satisfaction. *Qian* suggests the idea of a horse. *Kun*, that of an ox; *Zhen*, that of the dragon; *Xun*, that of a fowl; *Kan*, that of a pig; Li, that of a pheasant; *Gen*, that of a dog; and Dui, that of a sheep.

Qian suggests the idea of the head; *Kun*, that of the belly; *Zhen*, that of the feet; *Xun*, that of the thighs; *Kan*, that of the ears; *Li*, that of the eyes; *Gen*, that of the hands; and *Dui*, that of the mouth.

Qian is the symbol of heaven, and hence has the appellation of father. *Kun* is the symbol of earth, and hence has the appellation of mother. *Zhen* shows a first application of *Kun* to *Qian*, resulting in getting the first of its male or undivided lines, and hence is called 'the oldest son.'

● 乾爲馬、坤爲牛、震爲龍、巽爲雞、坎爲豕、離爲雉、艮爲狗、兌爲羊。

(以上 第八章)

● 乾爲首、坤爲腹、震爲足、巽爲股、坎爲耳、離爲目、艮爲手、兌爲口。

(以上 第九章)

● 乾、天也、故、稱乎父、坤、地也、故、稱乎母、震、一索而得男、故、謂之長男、巽、一索而得女、故、謂之長女、坎、再索而得男、故、謂之中男、離、再索而得女、故、謂之中女、艮、三索而得男、故、謂之少男、兌、三索而得女、故、謂之少女。(以上 第十章)

● 乾、爲天、爲圜、爲君、爲父、爲玉、爲金、爲寒、爲冰、爲大赤、爲良馬、爲老馬、爲瘠馬、爲駁馬、爲木果。○坤爲地、爲母、爲布、爲釜、爲吝嗇、爲均、爲子母牛、爲大輿、爲文、爲衆、爲柄、其於地也、爲黑。

● 震、爲雷、爲龍、爲玄黃、爲敷、爲大塗、爲長子、爲決躁、爲蒼筤竹、爲萑葦、其於馬也、爲善鳴、爲馵足、爲作足、爲的顙、其於稼也、爲反生、其究爲健、爲蕃鮮。

손巽은 첫 번째 구하여 딸을 얻은 것이니, 장녀長女라고 말하며, 감坎은 두번째 구하여 아들을 얻은 것이니, 중남中男이라 말하고, 이離는 두번째 구하여 딸을 얻은 것이니, 중녀中女라 말하며, 간艮은 세번째 구하여 아들을 얻은 것이니, 소남少男이라 말하고, 태兌는 세번째 구하여 딸을 얻은 것이니, 소녀少女라 말한다.
건乾은 하늘, 둥근 것, 임금, 아버지, 옥玉, 금金, 추위, 얼음, 크게 붉은 것, 좋은 말, 늙은 말, 마른 말, 얼룩말, 나무의 과실이 된다.
곤坤은 땅, 어머니, 포목, 가마솥, 인색함,

Xun shows a first application of *Qian* to *Kun*, resulting in getting the first of its female or divided lines, and hence is called 'the oldest daughter.' *Kan* shows a second application of *Kun* to *Qian*, resulting in getting the second of its male or undivided lines, and hence is called 'the second son.' *Li* shows a second application of *Qian* to *Kun*, resulting in getting the second of its female or divided lines, and hence is called 'the second daughter.' *Gen* shows a third application of *Kun* to *Qian*, resulting in getting the third of its male or undivided lines, and hence is called 'the youngest son.' *Dui* shows a third application of *Qian* to *Kun*, resulting in getting the third of its female or divided lines, and hence is called 'the youngest daughter.'
Qian suggests the idea of heaven; of a circle; of a ruler; of a father; of jade; of metal; of cold; of ice; of deep red; of a good horse; of an old horse; of a thin horse; of a piebald horse; and of the fruit of trees. *Kun* suggests the idea of the earth; of a mother; of cloth; of a caldron; of parsimony;

고른 것, 새끼 딸린 어미소, 큰 수레, 무늬, 무리, 자루, 땅에서는 검은 것이 된다.
진震은 우뢰, 용, 검고 누런 것, 펴는 것, 큰 길, 장자長子, 민첩하게 결단하는 것, 푸른 대나무, 갈대, 말에 있어서는 잘 우는 것, 왼발이 흰말, 발길질, 흰 이마, 심는 것에 있어서는 되생겨나는 것, 결국에는 굳셈이 되며, 번성하고 신선한 것이 된다.
손巽은 나무, 바람, 장녀長女, 먹줄, 장인, 흰색, 긴 것, 높은 것, 진퇴進退, 과단성果斷性이 없음, 냄새가 되며, 사람에 있어서는 털이 적은 것,

of a turning lathe; of a young heifer; of a large waggon; of what is variegated; of a multitude; and of a handle and support. Among soils it denotes what is black.
Zhen suggests the idea of thunder; of the dragon; of the union of the azure and the yellow; of development; of a great highway; of the eldest son; of decision and vehemence; of bright young bamboos; of sedges and rushes; among horses, of the good neigher; of one whose white hind-leg appears, of the prancer, and of one with a white star in his forehead. Among the productions of husbandry it suggests the idea of what returns to life from its disappearance beneath the surface, of what in the end becomes the strongest, and of what is the most luxuriant.
Xun suggests the idea of wood; of wind; of the oldest daughter; of a plumb-line; of a carpenter's square; of being white; of being long; of being lofty; of advancing and receding; of want of decision; and of strong scents. It suggests in the human body, the idea of deficiency of hair;

이마가 넓음, 눈에 흰자가 많음, 시장에서 3배에 가까운 이익을 얻으며, 결국에는 조급한 괘卦가 된다.
감坎은 물, 도랑, 숨어 엎드림, 굽은 것을 바로 잡음, 활과 바퀴가 되고, 사람에게 있어서는 근심을 더함, 심장병, 귀병, 혈괘血卦, 붉은 색이 되며, 말에 있어서는 아름다운 등, 급한 마음, 머리를 떨굼, 얇은 발꿈치, 끄는 말이 되고, 수레에 있어서는 병통이 많은 것이 되며, 통通함, 달, 도적이 된다. 나무에 있어서는 굳고 심이 많은 것이 된다.

of a wide forehead; of a large development of the white of the eye. Among tendencies, it suggests the close pursuit of gain, even to making three hundred per cent in the market. In the end it may become the trigram of decision.
Kan suggests the idea of water; of channels and ditches for draining and irrigation; of being hidden and lying concealed; of being now straight, and now crooked; of a bow, and of a wheel. As referred to man, it suggests the idea of an increase of anxiety; of distress of mind; of pain in the ears;—it is the trigram of the blood; it suggests the idea of what is red. As referred to horses, it suggests the idea of the horse with an elegant spine; of one with a high spirit; of one with a drooping head; of one with a thin hoof; and of one with a shambling step. As referred to carriages, it suggests one that encounters many risks. It suggests what goes right through; the moon; a thief. Referred to trees, it suggests that which is strong, and firm-hearted.

● 巽、爲木、爲風、爲長女、爲繩直、爲工、爲白、爲長、爲高、爲進退、爲不果、爲臭、其於人也、爲寡髮、爲廣顙、爲多白眼、爲近利市三倍、其究爲躁卦。

● 坎、爲水、爲溝瀆、爲隱伏、爲矯輮、爲弓輪、其於人也、爲加憂、爲心病、爲耳痛、爲血卦、爲赤、其於馬也爲美脊、爲亟心、爲下首、爲薄蹄、爲曳、其於輿也、爲多眚、爲通、爲月、爲盜、其於木也、爲堅多心。

● 離、爲火、爲日、爲電、爲中女、爲甲胄、爲戈兵、其於人也爲大腹、爲乾卦、爲鱉、爲蟹、爲蠃、爲蚌、爲龜、其於木也、爲科上槁。

● 艮、爲山、爲徑路、爲小石、爲門闕、爲果蓏、爲閽寺、爲指、爲狗、爲鼠、爲黔喙之屬、其於木也、爲堅多節。

● 兌、爲澤、爲少女、爲巫、爲口舌、爲毀折、爲附決、其於地也、爲剛鹵、爲妾爲羊。 (以上 第十一章)

이離는 불, 해, 번개, 중녀中女, 갑옷과 투구, 창과 군사가 되며, 사람에 있어서는 큰 배가 되고, 건괘乾卦, 자라, 게, 소라, 조개, 거북이 되며, 나무에 있어서는 속이 비고 마른 나무 끝이 된다.
간艮은 산, 지름길, 작은 돌, 대문, 과일 열매, 내시, 손가락, 개, 쥐, 부리가 검은 부류의 짐승이 되며, 그 나무에 있어서는 단단하고 마디가 많은 것이 된다.
태兌는 못, 소녀少女, 무당, 입과 혀, 헐고 끊어짐, 걸려서 찢어지는 것이 되며, 땅에 있어서는 굳고 짠 것이 되고, 첩妾, 양羊이 된다.

Li suggests the emblem of fire; oraint, there of lightning; of the second daughter; of buff-coat and helmet; of spear and sword. Referred to men, it suggests the large belly. It is the trigram of dryness. It suggests the emblem of a turtle; of a crab; of a spiral univalve; of the mussel; and of the tortoise. Referred to trees, it suggests one which is hollow and rotten above.
Gen suggests the emblem of a mountain; of a by-path; of a small rock; of a gateway; of the fruits of trees and creeping plants; of a porter or a eunuch; of the ring finger; of the dog; of the rat; of birds with powerful bills; among trees, of those which are strong, with many joints.
Dui suggests the emblem of a low-lying collection of water; of the youngest daughter; of a sorceress; of the mouth and tongue; of the decay and putting down of things in harvest; of the removal of fruits hanging from the stems or branches; among soils, of what is strong and salt; of a concubine; and of a sheep.

●有天地然後、萬物、生焉、○盈天地之間者、唯萬物。故、受之以屯。屯者盈也、屯者、物之始生也。○物生必蒙、故、受之以蒙、○蒙者、蒙也、物之穉也、物穉不可不養也。故、受之以需、需者、飲食之道也。○飲食必有訟、故、受之以訟。

●訟、必有衆起、故、受之以師。師者、衆也、衆必有所比、故、受之以比。

●比者、比也、比必有所畜、故、受之以小畜。物畜然後、有禮、故、受之以履。○履而泰然後、安、故、受之以泰。○泰者、通也、物不可以終通、故、受之以否。

●物不可以終否、故、受之以同人。與人同者、物必歸焉、故、受之以大有。

●有大者、不可以盈、故、受之以謙。○有大而能謙、必豫、故、受之以豫。

●豫必有隨、故、受之以隨。以喜隨人者必有事、故、受之以蠱。蠱者事也。

●有事而後、可大、故、受之以臨。○臨者、大也、○物大然後、可觀、故、受之以觀。○可觀而後、有所合、故、受之以噬嗑。○嗑者合也、物不可以苟合而已、故、受之以賁。賁者飾也、致飾然後、亨則盡矣、故、受之以剝。○剝者、剝也、物不可以終盡、剝、窮上反下、故、受之以復。

천지가 있은 뒤에 만물이 생겨나니, 하늘과 땅 사이에 가득찬 것은 오직 만물이다. 그러므로 건곤괘乾坤卦 다음에 둔괘屯卦로 받는다. 둔屯은 가득 찬 것이니, 둔屯은 생물이 비로소 생기는 것이다. 만물이 다 처음 생겨나면 반드시 어리니, 그러므로 몽괘蒙卦로 받는다. 몽蒙은 어린 것이어서 생물이 어린 것이니, 어린 것은 기르지 않을 수 없다. 그러므로 수괘需卦로 받으니, 수需는 음식飮食의 도道이다. 음식에는 반드시 송사訟事가 있으니, 그러므로 송괘訟卦로 받는다.
송사訟事는 반드시 무리로 일어난다. 그러므로 사괘師卦로 받는다. 사師는 무리이니, 무리는 모이면 반드시 서로 친해지는 바가 있다.

When there were heaven and earth, then afterwards all things were produced. What fills up the space between heaven and earth are those all things. Hence *Qian* and *Kun* are followed by *Tun*. Tun denotes filling up. *Tun* is descriptive of things on their first production. When so produced, they are sure to be in an undeveloped condition. Hence *Tu*n is followed by *Meng*. *Meng* is descriptive of what is undeveloped,—the young of creatures and things. These in that state require to be nourished. Hence *Meng* is followed by *Xu*. *Xu* is descriptive of the way in which meat and drink come to be supplied. Over meat and drink there are sure to be contentions. Hence *Xu* is followed by Song.
Song is sure to cause the rising up of the multitudes; and hence it is followed by *Shi*. *Shi* has the signification of multitudes, and between multitudes there must be some bond of union.

그러므로 비괘比卦로 받는다. 비比는 친한 것이니 서로 사람이 친하면 반드시 쌓는 것이 있다. 그러므로 소축小畜으로써 받는다. 물건의 쌓음이 있은 연후에 예의禮儀가 있으니, 그러므로 이履로써 받고 예의를 이행履行하여 태평한 연후에 편안하니, 그러므로 태괘泰卦로써 받는다. 태泰는 통하는 것이니, 모든 사물은 끝까지 통하지는 못하니, 그러므로 비否로써 받는다.
사물은 끝까지 비색否塞할 수는 없으니, 그러므로 동인괘同人卦로 받는다. 사람으로 더불어 함께 하는 자는 물건이 반드시 돌아가니, 그러므로 대유괘大有卦로 받는다. 크게 가진 자는 교만해서는 안되니, 그러므로 겸괘謙卦로 받는다.

Hence it is followed by *Bi*, which denotes being attached to. Multitudes in union must be subjected to some restraint. Hence *Bi* is followed by *Xiaochu*. When things are subjected to restraint, there come to be rites of ceremony, and hence *Xiaochu* is followed by *Lu*. The treading on what is proper leads to Tai, which issues in a state of freedom and repose, and hence *Lu* is followed by *Tai*. *Tai* denotes things having free course. They cannot have that for ever, and hence it is followed by *Fou* denoting being shut up and restricted.
Things cannot for ever be shut up, and hence *Fou* is followed by *Tongren*. To him who cultivates union with men, things must come to belong, and hence *Tongren* is followed by *Dayou*. Those who have what is great should not allow in themselves the feeling of being full, and hence *Dayou* is followed by *Qian*.

크게 갖고도 능히 겸손하면 반드시 즐거우니, 그러므로 예괘豫卦로 받는다. 즐거우면 반드시 따름이 있으니, 그러므로 수괘隨卦로 받는다. 기쁨으로써 사람을 따르는 자에게는 반드시 일이 있으니, 그러므로 고괘蠱卦로 받는다. 고蠱는 일이다.
일이 있은 뒤에 커질 수 있으니, 그러므로 임괘臨卦로 받는다. 임臨은 큰 것이고, 사물이 큰 뒤에 볼 수 있다. 그러므로 관괘觀卦로 받고 본 연후에 합하는 바 있으니, 그러므로 서합괘噬嗑卦로 받는다. 서嗑는 합하는 것이고, 물건은 가히 구차하게 합할 수 만은 없으니, 그러므로 비괘賁卦로 받는다. 비賁는 꾸미는 것이고, 꾸밈을 이룬 연후에 형통함을 다한다. 그러므로 박괘剝卦로써 받는다.

When great possessions are associated with humility, there is sure to be pleasure and satisfaction; and hence *Qian* is followed by *Yu*. Where such complacency is awakened, he who causes it is sure to have followers. They who follow another are sure to have services to perform, and hence *Sui* is followed by *Gu*. *Gu* means the performance of services.
He who performs such services may afterwards become great, and hence *Gu* is followed by *Lin*. *Lin* means great. What is great draws forth contemplation, and hence *Lin* is followed by *Guan*. He who attracts contemplation will then bring about the union of others with himself, and hence *Guan* is followed by *Shihe*. *Shihe* means union. But things should not be united in a reckless or irregular way, and hence Shihe is followed by *Bi*. *Bi* denotes adorning. When ornamentation has been carried to the utmost, its progress comes to an end; and hence *Bi* is followed by *Bao*.

●復則不妄矣、故、受之以无妄。○有无妄然後、可畜、故、受之以大畜。

●物畜然後、可養、故、受之以頤。○頤者、養也、不養則不可動、故、受之以大過。○物不可以終過、故、受之以坎。○坎者、陷也、陷必有所麗、故、受之以離。離者、麗也。（以上 上篇）

●有天地然後、有萬物、有萬物然後、有男女、有男女然後、有夫婦、有夫婦然後、有父子、有父子然後、有君臣、有君臣然後、有上下、有上下然後、禮義有所錯。○夫婦之道、不可以不久也、故、受之以恒、○恒者、久也。

●物不可以久居其所、故、受之以遯。○遯者、退也、物不可以終遯、故、受之以大壯。○物不可以終壯、故、受之以晉。○晉者、進也、進必有所傷、故、受之以明夷。○夷者、傷也。

●傷於外者必反其家、故、受之以家人。○家道窮必乖、故、受之以睽。睽者、乖也、乖必有難、故、受之以蹇。○蹇者、難也、物不可以終難、故、受之以解。○解者、緩也、緩必有所失、故、受之以損。

박剝은 깎는 것이고, 사물이 다 끝나버리지 않는 것이니, 위에서 다하면 아래로 돌아오니, 그러므로 복괘復卦로 받는다.
회복하면 망녕되지 않으니, 그러므로 무망괘无妄卦로 받는다. 망녕됨이 없는 뒤에 쌓을 수 있으니, 그러므로 대축괘大畜卦로 받는다. 사물을 쌓은 뒤에 기를 수 있으니, 그러므로 이괘頤卦로써 받는다. 이頤로 기르는 것이고, 기르지 않으면 움직이지 못하니, 그러므로 대과괘大過卦로써 받는다. 사물이 끝내 지나칠 수 없으니, 그러므로 감괘坎卦로써 받는다. 감坎은 빠지는 것이고, 빠지면 반드시 걸리는 바가 있으니, 그러므로 이괘離卦로써 받는다. 이離는 걸리는 것이다.

Bao denotes decay and overthrow. Things cannot be done away for ever. When decadence and overthrow have completed their work at one end, redintegration commences at the other; and hence *Bao* is followed by *Fu*.
When the return thus indicated has taken place, we have not any rash disorder, and *Fu* is followed by *Wuwang*. Given the freedom from disorder and insincerity which this name denotes, there may be the accumulation of virtue, and *Wuwang* is followed by *Daxu*. Such accumulation having taken place, there will follow the nourishment of it; and hence *Daxu* is followed by *Yi*. *Yi* denotes nourishing. Without nourishment there could be no movement, and hence *Yi* is followed by *Daguo*. Things cannot for ever be in a state of extraordinary progress; and hence *Daguo* is followed by *Kan*. *Kan* denotes falling into peril. When one falls into peril, he is sure to attach himself to some person or thing; and hence *Kan* is followed by *Li*. *Li* denotes being attached, or adhering, to.

천지가 있은 뒤에 만물이 있고, 만물이 있은 뒤에 남녀가 있으며, 남녀가 있은 뒤에 부부가 있고 부부가 있은 뒤에 부자가 있으며, 부자가 있은 뒤에 군신君臣이 있고, 군신이 있은 뒤에 상하上下가 있으며, 상하가 있은 연후에 예의禮儀가 행해질 수 있다. 대저 부부夫婦의 도道는 오래가지 않을 수 으니, 그러므로 항괘恒卦로써 받고, 항恒은 오래 하는 것이다.
물건이 오랫동안 그 자리에 있지 못하니, 그러므로 둔괘遯卦로써 받는다. 둔遯은 물러가는 것이고, 물건이 끝내 물러갈 수만 없으니, 그러므로 대장괘大壯卦로써 받는다. 물건이 끝내 장성할 수만 없다. 그러므로 진괘晉卦로써 받는다.

Heaven and earth existing, all material things then got their existence. All material things having existence, afterwards there came male and female. From the existence of male and female there came afterwards husband and wife. From husband and wife there came father and son. From father and son there came ruler and minister. From ruler and minister there came high and low. When the distinction of high and low had existence, afterwards came the arrangements of propriety and righteousness. The rule for the relation of husband and wife is that it should be long-enduring. Hence *Xian* is followed by *Heng*. *Heng* denotes long enduring.
Things cannot long abide in the same place; and hence *Heng* is followed by *Dun*. *Dun* denotes withdrawing. Things cannot be for ever withdrawn; and hence *Dun* is succeeded by *Dazhuang*. Things cannot remain for ever simply in the state of vigour; and hence *Dazhuang* is succeeded by *Jin*.

진晉은 나아가는 것이고, 나아가면 반드시 상傷하는 바 있으니, 그러므로 명이괘明夷卦로써 받는다. 이夷는 상傷하는 것이다.
밖에서 상傷한 자는 반드시 그 집으로 돌아오니, 그러므로 가인괘家人卦로써 받는다. 가도家道가 궁하면 반드시 어긋난다. 그러므로 규괘睽卦로써 받는다. 규睽는 어긋나는 것이고, 어긋나면 반드시 어려움이 있으니, 그러므로 건괘蹇卦로써 받는다. 건蹇은 어려운 것이고, 사물이 끝내 어렵지는 않으니, 그러므로 해괘解卦로써 받는다. 해解는 늘어지는 것이고 늘어지면 반드시 잃는 바가 있으니, 그러므로 손괘損卦로써 받는다.
계속 덜어내면 반드시 더함이 있으니, 그러므로 익괘益卦로써 받는다.

Jin denotes advancing. But advancing is sure to lead to being wounded; and hence *Jin* is succeeded by *Mingyi*. I denotes being wounded. He who is wounded abroad will return to his home; and hence *Mingyi* is followed by *Jiaren*.
When the right administration of the family is at an end, misunderstanding and division will ensure; and hence *Jiaren* is followed by *Kui*. *Kui* denotes misunderstanding and division; and such a state is sure to give rise to difficulties and complications. *Kui* therefore is followed by *Jian*. *Jian* denotes difficulties; but things cannot remain for ever in such a state. *Jian* therefore is followed by *Jie*, which denotes relaxation and ease. In a state of relaxation and ease there are sure to be losses; and hence *Jie* is followed by *Sun*.
But when *Sun* or diminution is going on without end, increase is sure to come. *Sun* therefore is followed by *Yi*.

● 損而不已、必益、故、受之以益。○益而不已、必決、故、受之以夬。

● 夬者、決也、決必有遇、故、受之以姤。○姤者、遇也、物相遇而後、聚、故、受之以萃。萃者、聚也、聚而上者、謂之升、故、受之以升。○升而不已、必困、故、受之以困。

● 困乎上者必反下、故、受之以井。○井道不可不革、故、受之以革。○革物者、莫若鼎、故、受之以鼎。○主器者莫若長子、故、受之以震。○震者、動也、物不可以終動、止之、故、受之以艮。○艮者、止也、物不可以終止、故、受之以漸。○漸者、進也、進必有所歸、故、受之以歸妹。○得其所歸者必大、故、受之以豐。○豐者、大也。

● 窮大者必失其居、故、受之以旅。○旅而无所容、故、受之以巽。○巽者、入也、入而後、說之、故、受之以兌。○兌者、說也、說而後、散之、故、受之以渙。渙者、離也、物不可以終離、故、受之以節。○節而信之、故、受之以中孚。有其信者、必行之、故、受之以小過。○有過物者、必濟、故、受之以既濟。○物不可窮也、故、受之以未濟、終焉。(以上 下篇)

계속 더하면 반드시 터지니, 그러므로 쾌괘夬卦로써 받는다. 쾌夬는 결단함이고, 결단함에 반드시 만나는 바가 있으니, 그러므로 구괘姤卦로써 받는다. 구姤는 만남이고 사물이 서로 만난 뒤에 모이니, 그러므로 취괘萃卦로써 받는다. 취萃는 모이는 것이고 모여서 오르는 것을 승升이라 말하니, 그러므로 승괘升卦로써 받는다. 계속 올라가면 반드시 곤궁해지니, 그러므로 곤괘困卦로써 받는다.
위에서 곤궁한 자는 반드시 아래로 돌아오니, 그러므로 정괘井卦로써 받는다. 우물의 도道는 고치지 않을 수 없으니, 그러므로 혁괘革卦로써 받는다.

When increase goes on without end, there is sure to come a dispersing of it, and hence *Yi* is followed by *Guai*. *Guai* denotes dispersion. But dispersion must be succeeded by a meeting again. Hence *Guai* is followed by *Gou*, which denotes such meeting. When things meet together, a collection is then formed. Hence *Gou* is followed by *Cui*, which name denotes being collected. When good men are collected and mount to the highest places, there results what we call an upward advance; and hence *Cui* is followed by *Sheng*. When such advance continues without stopping, there is sure to come distress; and hence *Sheng* is followed by Kun.
When distress is felt in the height that has been gained, there is sure to be a return to the ground beneath; and hence *Kun* is followed by *Jing*. What happens under *Jing* requires to be changed, and hence it is followed by *Ge* denoting change.

사물을 고치는 것은 솥만한 것이 없으니, 그러므로 정괘鼎卦로써 받는다. 그릇을 맡은 자는 장자만한 이가 없으니, 그러므로 진괘震卦로써 받는다. 진震은 움직이는 것이고, 사물이 끝내 움직여서 그치게 되니, 그러므로 간괘艮卦로써 받는다. 간艮은 그치는 것이고, 사물이 마침내 그치지는 못하니, 그러므로 점괘漸卦로 받는다. 점漸은 나가는 것이고, 나가면 반드시 돌아가는 바가 있으니, 그러므로 귀매괘歸妹卦로써 받는다. 그 돌아갈 바를 얻은 자는 반드시 커지게 되니, 그러므로 풍괘豐卦로써 받는다. 풍豐은 큰 것이다.
큰 것을 다하면 반드시 거소居所를 잃으니, 그러므로 여괘旅卦로써 받는다.

For changing the substance of things there is nothing equal to the caldron; and hence *Ge* is followed by *Ding*. For presiding over that and all other vessels, no one is equal to the eldest son, and hence Ding is followed by *Zhen*. *Zhen* conveys the idea of putting in motion. But things cannot be kept in motion for ever. The motion is stopped; and hence *Zhen* is followed by *Gen*, which gives the idea of arresting or stopping. Things cannot be kept for ever in a state of repression, and hence *Gen* is followed by *Jian*, which gives the idea of gradually advancing. With advance there must be a certain point that is arrived at, and hence *Jian* is succeeded by *Guimei*. When things thus find the proper point to which to come, they are sure to become great. Hence *Guimei* is succeeded by *Li*, which conveys the idea of being great.
He whose greatness reaches the utmost possibility, is sure to lose his dwelling; and hence *Li* is succeeded by *Lu* denoting travellers or strangers.

나그네는 받아주는 데가 없으니, 그러므로 손괘巽卦로써 받는다. 손巽은 들어가는 것이고, 들어간 뒤에 기뻐하니, 그러므로 태괘兌卦로써 받는다. 태兌는 기뻐하는 것이고, 기뻐한 뒤에 흩어지니, 그러므로 환괘渙卦로써 받는다. 환渙은 떠나는 것이고, 사물이 끝내 떠나가 버릴수 만은 없으니, 그러므로 절괘節卦로써 받는다. 절도가 있어서 믿으니, 그러므로 중부괘中孚卦로써 받는다. 그 믿음이 있는 자는 반드시 행하니, 그러므로 소과괘小過卦로써 받는다. 다른 사물보다 지나치는 자는 반드시 일을 마무리 지으니, 그러므로 기제괘旣濟卦로써 받는다. 사물이 다 끝날 수는 없으니, 그러므로 미제괘未濟卦로써 받아서 마친다.

We have in it the idea of strangers who have no place to receive them, and hence *Lu* is followed by *Xun*, which gives the idea of penetrating and entering. One enters on the pursuit of his object, and afterwards has pleasure in it; hence *Xun* is followed by *Dui*. *Dui* denotes pleasure and satisfaction. This pleasure and satisfaction begins afterwards to be dissipated, and hence *Dui* is followed by *Huan*, which denotes separation and division. A state of division cannot continue for ever, and therefore *Huan* is followed by *Jie*. *Jie* or the system of regulations having been established, men believe in it, and hence it is followed by *Zhongfu*. When men have the belief which *Zhongfu* implies, they are sure to carry it into practice; and hence it is succeeded by *Xiaoguo*. He that surpasses others is sure to remedy evils that exist, and therefore *Xiaoguo* is succeeded by *Jiji*. But the succession of events cannot come to an end, and therefore *Jiji* is succeeded by *Weiji*, with which the hexagrams come to a close.

雜卦傳

●乾剛坤柔、○比樂師憂、○臨觀之義、或與或求。○屯、見而不失其居、蒙、雜而著。○震、起也、艮、止也、損益、盛衰之始也。○大畜、時也、无妄、災也。○萃、聚而升、不來也、○謙、輕而豫、怠也。○噬嗑、食也、賁、无色也、○兌、見而巽、伏也。○隨、无故也、蠱則飭也。

●剝、爛也、復、反也。○晉、晝也、明夷、誅也。○井、通而困、相遇也。○咸、速也、恒、久也。○渙、離也、節、止也。○解、緩也、蹇、難也。○睽、外也、家人、內也。○否泰、反其類也。○大壯則止、遯則退也。○大有、衆也、同人、親也。○革、去故也、鼎、取新也。○小過、過也、中孚、信也。豐、多故。親寡、旅也、○離、上而坎、下也。小畜、寡也、履、不處也。

●需、不進也、訟、不親也。○大過、顚也、○姤、遇也、柔遇剛也。漸、女歸、待男行也。○頤、養正也、○旣濟、定也。○歸妹、女之終也、

●未濟、男之窮也。夬、決也、剛決柔也。君子道長、小人道憂也。

건乾은 강하고 곤坤은 부드러우며, 비比는 즐겁고 사師는 근심한다. 임臨과 관觀의 뜻은 주거나 구하는 것이다. 둔屯은 나타나서 그 있을 곳을 잃지 않는 것이요, 몽蒙은 섞여서 나타나는 것이다. 진震은 일어나는 것이요, 간艮은 그치는 것이다. 손損과 익益은 성함과 쇠함이 시작되는 것이다. 대축大畜은 때요, 무망无妄은 재앙이다. 췌萃는 모으는 것이고, 승升은 오지 않는 것이며, 겸謙은 가벼운 것이고, 예豫는 게으른 것이다. 서합噬嗑은 먹는 것이고, 비賁는 색깔이 없는 것이며, 태兌는 나타나는 것이요, 손巽은 엎드리는 것이다. 수隨는 연고가 없는 것이요, 고蠱는 가지런히 다스리는 것이다.

Strength in *Qian*, weakness in *Kun* we find. *Bi* shows us joy, and *Shi* the anxious mind. Lin gives, *Guan* seeks;—such are the several themes Their different figures were to teach designed. *Tun* manifests itself, yet keeps its place; 'Mid darkness still, to light *Meng* sets its face. *Zhen* starts; *Gen* stops. In Sun and *Yi* are seen.

How fulness and decay their course begin. *Daxu* keeps still, and waits the proper time. *Wuwang* sets forth how evil springs from crime. Good men in *Cui* collect; in *Sheng* they rise: *Qian* itself, *Yu* others doth despise. *Shike* takes eating for its theme; and *Bi* Takes what is plain, from ornament quite free. *Dui* shows its scope, but Sun's we do not see. *Sui* quits the old; *Gu* makes a new decree.

박剝은 무르익어 떨어지는 것이요, 복復은 돌아오는 것이다. 진晉은 낮이요 명이明夷는 베는 것이다. 정井은 통하는 것이요, 곤困은 서로 만나는 것이다. 함咸은 빠른 것이요, 항恒은 오래된 것이다. 환渙은 떠나는 것이요, 절節은 그치는 것이다. 해解는 풀어주는 것이요, 건蹇은 어려운 것이다. 규睽는 밖이요, 가인家人은 안이다. 비否와 태泰는 그 종류를 반대하는 것이다. 대장大壯은 그치는 것이요, 둔遯은 물러가는 것이다. 대유大有는 무리요, 동인同人은 친함이다. 혁革은 옛 것을 버리는 것이요, 정鼎은 새것을 취하는 것이다. 소과小過는 지나침이요, 중부中孚는 믿는 것이다. 풍豊은 연고가 많은 것이요, 친한 이가 적은 것은 나그네다.

We see in *Bao* its subject worn away; And *Fu* shows its recovering from decay. Above in *Jin* the sun shines clear and bright, But in *Mingyi* 'tis hidden from the sight. Progress in *Jing* in Kun encounters blight. Effect quick answering cause in *xian* appears; While *Heng* denotes continuance for years. *Huan* scatters; but *Jie* its code of rules uprears. Relief and ease with *Jie* are sure to come; Hard toil and danger have in *Jian* their home. *Kui* looks on others as beyond its care; *Jiaren* all includes within its sphere. While *Fou* and *Tai* their different scopes prefer, *Dazhuang* stops here as right; withdraws *Dun* there. *Dayou* adhering multitudes can show; *Tongren* reflects their warm affection's glow. Ding takes what's new; the old is left by *Ge*. Sincere is *Zhongfu*; but exceeds, *xiaoguo*. *Li* tells of trouble; *Lu* can boast few friends.

이離는 위고 감坎은 아래이다. 소축小畜은 적은 것이요, 이履는 거처하지 않는 것이다.
수需는 나아가지 않는 것이요, 송訟은 친근하지 않은 것이다. 대과大過는 넘어지는 것이고, 구姤는 만남이며, 유柔가 강剛을 만남이다. 점漸은 여자가 시집을 감에 남자를 기다려 가는 것이다. 이頤는 바른 것을 기르는 것이요, 기제旣濟는 정하는 것이다. 귀매歸妹는 여자의 마침이요, 미제未濟는 남자의 궁함이다. 쾌夬는 결단함이요 강剛은 유柔를 결단하는 것이다. 군자의 도道는 커지고 소인의 도道는 걱정스럽게 된다.

Fire mounts in *Li*; water in *Kan* descends. *xiaochu* with few 'gainst many foes contends. Movement in *Lu*, unresting, never ends.
Xu shows its subject making no advance: In Song we seek in vain a friendly glance; And *Daguo's* overthrown with sad mischance. *Gou* shows a meeting, where the many strong Are met by one that's weak, yet struggles long. In *Jian* we see a bride who will delay To move until the bridegroom takes his way. Body and mind are nourished right in *Yi*; All things are well established in *Jiji*. *Guimei* reveals how ends the virgin life; *Weiji* how fails the youth to get a wife. The strong disperse the weak; *Guai* teaches so. Prospers the good man's way; to grief all small men go.

주역(周易) 대구한의대학교출판부